"In his luminous prose, Tom Steagald leads readers through the Christian year from Advent to Christ the King, weaving together fresh telling of the ancient story and poignant personal experience and observation. This little book is a find for all ready to walk through the liturgical calendar looking for new treasure hidden in the familiar."

—MICHAEL L. LINDVALL, author of *A Geography of God*

"Steagald sounds the melody of God's story and then dovetails in the counterpoint of personal experience with both lines of notes hung on the staff of the Christian liturgical year. A fascinating approach."

—JAMES C. HOWELL, PhD, senior pastor, Myers Park United Methodist Church, Charlotte, North Carolina; author of twelve books, including *The Beatitudes for Today* and *Yours Are the Hands of Christ*

"Steagald takes us on a journey with Jesus—a journey that is both familiar and fresh."

—DAVID HOWELL, editor, Lectionary Homiletics

"If we are going to follow Jesus, we will pay attention to the paths of righteousness that are set before us. Yet at times we are unclear about the traveling conditions, much less the destination. Tom Steagald has a gift for describing the spiritual journey of discipleship, helping us not only to discern where we are at each step along the way but also to envision the future with hope and confidence."

—DR. KEN CARTER, pastor; author of *A Way of Life in the World*

"If you have ever longed to follow Jesus (or help others do so), read *Every Disciple's Journey*. Steagald skillfully retells the story of Jesus within the framework of the Christian calendar. Blending theological reflection, personal experience, and the insights of an experienced pastor, he prods us to move from self-centered to God-centered faith."

—MICHAEL A. SMITH, PhD, senior pastor, First Baptist Church, Murfreesboro, Tennessee

"Tom Steagald is a brother in Christ who joyfully and humbly admits to the miraculous transformation wrought by God's grace. This book is not so much the testimony of one who has arrived as it is the journal of an enthusiastic and earnest pilgrim seeking on bent and often aching knees to follow Christ higher up and further in. Reader, journey with him through the seasons of the year and of life, Bible open in hand and heart open before God. You will be blesse

—REVEREND  tor, ado

"Tom Steagald packs this book with valuable resources for those beginning or already embarked on the quest to follow Jesus. He offers a delightful and imaginative retelling of key gospel stories in a setting that serves as an introduction and exploration of the liturgical calendar. The insertion of valuable theological insights and provocative questions makes it a book well worth reading."

EVERY DISCIPLE'S JOURNEY

FOLLOWING JESUS TO A GOD-FOCUSED FAITH

THOMAS R. STEAGALD

NAVPRESS®

OUR GUARANTEE TO YOU

We believe so strongly in the message of our books that we are making this quality guarantee to you. If for any reason you are disappointed with the content of this book, return the title page to us with your name and address and we will refund to you the list price of the book. To help us serve you better, please briefly describe why you were disappointed. Mail your refund request to: NavPress, P.O. Box 35002, Colorado Springs, CO 80935.

The Navigators is an international Christian organization. Our mission is to advance the gospel of Jesus and His kingdom into the nations through spiritual generations of laborers living and discipling among the lost. We see a vital movement of the gospel, fueled by prevailing prayer, flowing freely through relational networks and out into the nations where workers for the kingdom are next door to everywhere.

NavPress is the publishing ministry of The Navigators. The mission of NavPress is to reach, disciple, and equip people to know Christ and make Him known by publishing life-related materials that are biblically rooted and culturally relevant. Our vision is to stimulate spiritual transformation through every product we publish.

ISBN-13: 978-1-57683-880-8
ISBN-10: 1-57683-880-3

Cover design by studiogearbox.com
Cover image by Steve Gardner/PixelWorks
Creative Team: Terry Behimer, Liz Heaney, Bruce Casson, Kathy Mosier, Arvid Wallen, Kathy Guist

Some of the anecdotal illustrations in this book are true to life and are included with the permission of the persons involved. All other illustrations are composites of real situations, and any resemblance to people living or dead is coincidental.

Most of the definitions given throughout this book are taken from Merriam-Webster OnLine, http://www .m-w.com/.

Unless otherwise identified, all Scripture quotations in this publication are taken from the *Revised Standard Version Bible* (RSV), copyright 1946, 1952, 1971, by the Division of Christian Education of the National Council of the Churches of Christ in the USA, used by permission, all rights reserved. Other versions used include the *New Revised Standard Version* (NRSV), copyright © 1989, by the Division of Christian Education of the National Council of the Churches of Christ in the USA, used by permission, all rights reserved; the *New King James Version* (NKJV). Copyright © 1982 by Thomas Nelson, Inc. Used by permission. All rights reserved; and the *King James Version* (KJV).

Steagald, Tom.
  Every disciple's journey : following Jesus to a God-focused faith /
Thomas R. Steagald.
    p. cm.
  Includes bibliographical references.
  ISBN-13: 978-1-57683-880-8
  ISBN-10: 1-57683-880-3
  1. Jesus Christ--Biography. 2. Church year meditations. 3.
Spirituality--Christianity. I. Title.
BT301.3.S74 2007
242'.3--dc22
                              2007016463

Printed in the United States of America

1 2 3 4 5 6 7 8 / 11 10 09 08 07

FOR A FREE CATALOG OF NAVPRESS BOOKS & BIBLE STUDIES,
CALL 1-800-366-7788 (USA) OR 1-800-839-4769 (CANADA).

For Ray Lassister Steagald

(1916–1988)

simul justus et peccator,

who believed in spite of himself and at the last, by grace,

received all he had long promised to others.

"Those who love their life lose it, and those who hate

their life in this world will keep it for eternal life."

(John 12:25, NRSV)

The liturgical calendar as a whole exists in large part to remind us that Christ has sanctified all of time, bringing the whole of our experience into the orbit of resurrection. What we deem ordinary, God has transformed into the extraordinary by the power of divine grace.

— LAURENCE HULL STOOKEY,
Calendar: Christ's Time for the Church

Contents

Acknowledgments

What does anyone who speaks of you really say? Yet woe betide those who fail to speak while the chatterboxes go on saying nothing.

— Saint Augustine, *The Confessions*, BOOK 1, PARAGRAPH 4

Saint Augustine, bishop of Hippo and Doctor of the Church, long ago prayed that prayer. All these centuries later I find deep resonance in his confession; he states far better than I could the ambivalence I feel as I preface this, yet another book on Jesus.

I know better than anyone else that I have said nothing new. What *new*, really, is there to say? And how dare I? I am no scholar or wise man. My elders and betters have more eloquently told many of these same stories, have offered many of these same insights, have asked and even answered many of these same questions. Perhaps I should have just stayed my hand and kept my heart and mouth shut.

But I also know the demand of the subject. Like the prophets (if only in this way), like apostles and martyrs, like saints both windowed and nameless, like my professors and pastors and Sunday school teachers—and like my own father not least—I know the burning that comes with not speaking. I know the fire in one's bones that compels testimony, no matter how inadequate it may prove to be.

So within the limits set by my experience and awareness, I have tried to muster the best words I could to tell the "old, old Story" in hopes that it will come to life again in the hearing of the reader. I know that such a result is properly the work of the Holy Spirit; I only hope, following the recent counsel of Amy-Jill Levine, I have given the Holy Spirit something to work with.

Phillips Brooks defined preaching as "truth through personality." This definition is too pristine by half, but in any case it is more or less what happens Sunday by Sunday. Truth, or something akin to it, is refracted through the experiences and disposition of the preacher so as to be fleshed out in words and gesture. It is a solitary task in many ways, even a lonely one, preparing this most public expression of one's call to ministry. I'm thankful that preaching is done "in the midst," in a congregation who, by grace, can turn the loneliness into community and the preaching itself into dialogue.

Writing, too, may share with preaching both the burden of solitude and the (potential) joy of community. I am so very thankful to have been blessed, twice now, to live and work—not geographically but relationally—among a group of interested others who have taken my reflections and introspections as cues for genuine conversation.

I will try not to blather on.

Thanks especially to my wife, Jo, and to our kids not a little, who in their own ways endured with great patience and good humor not only my long stretches of reclusion but also my increasing levels of anxiety and irritation, sleepless worry, and grumpiness when I could not for the life of me get the toothpaste into the tube.

Thanks also to Tabitha, my delightful secretary, who warded me with fierce loyalty over long weeks. Thanks—such deep and abiding thanks—to my wonderful parishioners at First United Methodist Church in Stanley, North Carolina. They gave me gifts not only of space and time—no small matters—but also their belief in and even celebration of this sometimes isolating and time-consuming aspect of my ministry. Thanks to Sheila, who, God bless her, sent me flowers and a balloon when I *finally* finished.

Thanks to Poke and Jill for the use of their mountain condominium.

Thanks to Mike, Larry, Doris, and Lori for reading early sections of the manuscript. Even more thanks to Jo, who not only read the many drafts but even proofed them—over and over and over again—even when much of what she read eventually found its way (rightly) into the trash.

Thanks to Bob for his help on John 12.

Thanks to Rachelle for offering me a contract.

And thanks most especially to Liz, my editor and my friend. She loved me enough to tell me what I was doing wasn't working, and then she stayed right there to help me find what might. She demanded that I do better and applauded when at last I did. She coached, prodded, and almost fussed once or twice. She made me rethink and clarify, delete and rewrite, show rather than tell, and do the hard work that passes for art. I owe Liz more than I can ever repay.

The book is dedicated to my father, God rest his weary soul. Indeed, that is my prayer. Dad could be difficult and many times was, a man at war with lots of things and mostly himself. He was a bundle of contradictions and self-loathing. His heart contracted, Grinch-like I think, through the years; Dad gave till it hurt. But he was needy and petulant too, self-absorbed and sullen. On good days he had a great laugh and a wonderful sense of humor; on bad days he excoriated even those who loved him best. He sequestered himself in his illnesses, his disappointments, his guilt and regrets. His life did not turn out as he had expected.

It was on his prayer-flattened knee, however, that I asked Jesus into my heart. It was on long drives to a small country church he served when I was eight or nine that he became my first instructor in the faith. His sermons were the first I ever heard preached and his prayers the first I ever heard prayed. I love the Bible because of Dad, and I am a pastor in part because I heard his call as clearly as I heard Jesus'. I am thankful for him, hard as he was, and I am comforted to think that his death granted him both healing and, if not forgetfulness, then peace when, very early one late Advent morning, Jesus opened the door to a life Dad had sometimes preached but had not even begun to fully imagine.

When I wrote my first little book, Dad autographed copies of it and gave them to some of his buddies. Back then I was annoyed; now I can only hope he would do the same with this one.

Jesus Calls, Disciples Follow

Wherever He leads, I'll go.

—B. B. McKinney

Jesus comes to the shore of the Sea of Galilee, as perhaps He's come many times before. This time, though, He stops near two fishermen, Simon and Andrew, who are casting their nets into the shallow waters. "Follow me," He says. Maybe they know who He is—have seen Him on the shore other days, heard Him preach in the synagogue, had conversation enough to recognize His urgent and authoritative voice—or maybe not. Either way, the two men drop their nets, wade out of the shallows, and follow Him.

A little farther up the shore Jesus stops near a boat. It belongs to old Zebedee, but soon it will belong to Zebedee's two sons, when his own fishing days are over. He will give them the boats and the business, the hired hands and his private map of all the best fishing spots. He will settle down to enjoy his retirement, his grandchildren. But on this day Jesus stops at Zebedee's boat. Two other men pause with Jesus, huddling a ways behind, former fishermen themselves. Jesus calls to Zebedee's sons, James and John, much the same way He called to Simon and Andrew, and the old man can only watch as, in a heartbeat, all his plans change.

Did Jesus call anyone else that day? Any of the servants, or even old Zebedee himself? We don't know. But Jesus did call James and John, who up and left their father and the boat and the nets and the servants. They fell in with Simon and Andrew, following after Jesus. Did Zebedee bless them as they went or curse them, his heart, like his imagined future, breaking as a wave on the shore? Did he have the first idea what his sons were doing? No more than they, I suppose, but we can only speculate. All we know for sure is that now there are five sets of footprints on the sand where there had been only one.

Frame the moment, the picture: Jesus comes to the fishermen, right where they are standing, and calls to them. They answer, the first of many men and women who do, and off they go. They go because Jesus called. They walk with Him *away* from the Sea of Galilee because He came *to* the Sea of Galilee seeking disciples. The steps they take are a response of faith; His are the initiative of grace. God loves. Jesus calls. Disciples follow. These fishermen go with Jesus, do not want the big one to get away.

Every disciple's journey begins with answering Jesus, and answering Jesus always means following Him step-by-step wherever He leads. While those first disciples did not know where that might be, what those new places and situations might demand, they worked hard to keep pace.

"Follow me" is never an easy command to obey. At the very least it's hard on the feet, for discipleship often means going with Jesus from place to place. He does not stay long anywhere but is always moving on to the next town, the next synagogue, the next need. Discipleship is harder yet on the ears and the head and hardest of all on the heart, whose highways are built over mountainous rationalizations, gouged deep by storms of selfishness, pocked with cynicism and self-doubt.

But "make his path straight," the prophet cries,[1] and we believe he means in the world and also in us. By God's own word all the mountains will be flattened and the valleys filled up—all the rough places smoothed—that the Lord might come to us and we in turn might follow Him as on level ground.[2] Jesus seeks to enlist us in God's work in the world, calls us to learn God's ways and God's will, trains us for service as God's emissaries.

A disciple is, by definition, a student, one who follows. Disciples of Jesus are those who have chosen to follow Him, whether geographically—as in the case of Simon and Matthew, James, John, and the others—or otherwise, as is the case for most of the rest of us. While some of Jesus' disciples still follow Him from home to other places of service, all of His disciples seek to journey from a self-centered faith toward a God-centered faith.

This book sets about to help us negotiate that journey, or at least part of it. I make use of the Christian year (the Temporal Cycle, as it is sometimes called) as a kind of map. The seasons of the Christian year—from Advent through Christ the King—constitute the Church's traditional way of telling the story of Jesus' life and also suggest an implicit itinerary for our journey with Him. As we recount Jesus' movements, season to season, we will affirm certain aspects of His life and work. Those affirmations will prompt confession that because we often remain self-focused, as individuals and as a Church, we have often failed to go where Jesus goes, to do what Jesus does. But with confession comes the opportunity for repentance and renewed dedication to go wherever Jesus leads.

But why use the Christian year as a map?

Jesus is God's will and Word made flesh.[3] Reflecting on His ministry and miracles, His teaching and suffering, His death, resurrection, and abiding presence, His once and future reign, helps us learn how to be better disciples. We follow Him, imitate Him, begin to let our flesh incarnate His Word and will as more and more we come to "see him as he is."[4]

Week by week, year by year, a patterned reading of the Gospels recounts both Jesus' life and His claim on the disciples who chose to follow Him. The "seasons" of His life proclaim that Jesus is the Light of the World (Advent), born both King of the Jews (Christmas) and Savior of the world (Epiphany). His saving work will occasion resistance and suffering (Lent) and lead eventually to His death (Holy Week and Good Friday). But death is not the last word (Easter

Day), and both in His person and in the sending of the Holy Spirit, Jesus gives life and memory and power to His disciples (Easter season and Pentecost).

Many branches of the Christian family worship according to this seasonal rhythm, not only to herald those truths, but also to confess that our own concerns are narrower than our summons—that we are in the dark still, that we are parochial in our perspective, loathe to suffer, and minimalist in our understanding of Resurrection and Spirit. The value of the Christian year, then, is both pastoral and practical, both historic and contemporary.

There is also a prophetic aspect to observing the Temporal Cycle, for it is part of our fallen nature that we pick and choose what we like best about Jesus and the Gospels and ignore or discount the rest. As Lauren Winner has recently noted, many godly and well-meaning people have unwittingly taught recent generations of believers to read the Bible only in snippets, without a sense of the great narrative sweep of Scripture or our own part in the Story.[5] Contemporary preaching has also deepened the crisis. In many of our congregations we hear mostly "how-to" sermons, often founded on small portions of Scripture and forced into mechanistic formulas to offer easy political, moral, or even financial lessons.

Engaging the more comprehensive drama of the gospel may let the scales fall from the eyes of our preconceptions and help us recognize Jesus at last. Recalling the fuller life and ministry of Jesus by means of the Christian year helps us avoid the kind of fragmentation and gnostic disembodiment that can occur when we recall only our favorite stories or read our three-minute devotionals. The Temporal Cycle paints it all again year after year, the whole life and ministry of Jesus, His coming and call in all its fullness, which is our best guide to discipleship.

All preaching and teaching, of course—and even books such as this—do *some* picking and choosing. We cannot tell every story every time. But if we always keep before us the comprehensive sweep of Jesus' life, we will not so easily caricature the One whose Story we attempt to tell.

By means of midrash, mostly—biblical and theological reflections—but with a bit of memoir too, I will tell the Story. I hope, along the way, to help readers find not only new insights for reading the texts but also new ways to navigate the distance from head to heart and to live their faith more authentically.

Thomas R. Steagald
Epiphany 2007

PART ONE

GOD'S JOURNEY TO US

Advent [Middle English, from Medieval Latin *adventus*, from Latin, arrival, from *advenire*] **1:** the period beginning four Sundays before Christmas and observed by some Christians as a season of prayer and fasting **2a:** the coming of Christ at the Incarnation

Christmas

Epiphany

Lent

Holy Week

Easter

Pentecost

Trinity

Ordinary Time

Christ the King

Chapter 1

Promises in the Dark

Advent

O come, O come, Emmanuel, and ransom captive Israel,
That mourns in lonely exile here, until the Son of God
    appear.
Rejoice! Rejoice! Emmanuel shall come to thee, O Israel.

— NINTH-CENTURY LATIN HYMN

Come, Thou Long-Expected Jesus, born to set thy people
    free;
From our fears and sins release us, let us find our rest in thee.
Israel's strength and consolation, hope of all the earth thou
    art;
Dear Desire of every nation, joy of every longing heart.

— CHARLES WESLEY

Does anyone believe the galaxies exist to add splendor to the
night sky over Bethlehem?

— ANNIE DILLARD

In the beginning, when God created the heavens and the earth, there was nothing but darkness, chaos, and void. God hovered over the face of the deep, silenced the howl of confusion, filled the emptiness with His will and word: "Let there be light," God said, and there was light. Not many days later there was more than that, land and sea and life enough to fill them both. The darkness remained a part of things, of course, but confined and partitioned—the dusk itself serving as a kind of overture for the dawn.

Those who first told us the story of our beginnings always began with the evening—that was the beginning of every new day.[1] Creation itself began in the darkness, and whenever darkness gathers, there is a black velvet canvas on which God may paint light and mercy—morning by morning, so great is God's faithfulness[2]—a great, closed curtain to be pulled back yet again to reveal the next blessed dawn.

There were evenings, there were mornings, and it was good.

At week's end God knelt in the Good Garden, scooped damp earth into His hands and worked it, molded and shaped something quite unlike anything He had yet made. God then breathed into *Adam* His own misty breath, and the dirt came alive with the life of God. God stood—sweat streaking His cheeks, Eden staining His knees, satisfaction relaxing His brow—and brushed His hands together in order to wipe off the last bits of His work's remains.

The Man, God's fingerprints all over him, coughed and rose, squinted into his first awareness of the Good Garden, awakened to his first dim notions of the Good Gardener. Soon there was Woman and the prospect of offspring, and it was all of it so very good, the heavens and the earth, that God rested.

And then all Hell broke loose. The darkness whelmed its partition, surged over into every place and thing, every thought and motive. Night now signaled the end, not the beginning. When the Man and the Woman broke the lone command God had given them, the sun dimmed and so did the Man and the Woman's vision. Darker still grew the countenance of their firstborn against his younger brother —there was envy and there was murder and it was all of it very bad—and soon not only the children of the earth but even the earth itself languished and mourned. The only clear light radiated from the angel's flaming sword. Thorns choked the flowers and fields.

The children of the earth were fruitful but withered, deformed almost beyond recognition. They multiplied but were diminished, weakened, no longer able to subdue the earth or even enjoy it completely. Instead, they used the earth, were punished by it, tilled it in uneasy truce. The Good Garden became a bad and lonely place as the Man, the Woman, and all their unfortunate offspring nearly forgot the intimacy God had made them for and instead spent their days isolated, segregated, fearful. The children of the earth rebelled against their Maker, tried to deny both God's image and His word. They ignored God's fingerprints on them, spurned God's counsel, maintained that both were fictions forced on the naive.

In most of our own generation the rebellion continues unabated, either in active disobedience or thoughtless disregard. Like the Man and the Woman before us, we find ourselves in terrified exile from we are not sure what. Squinting, not for the splendor of the light anymore but on account of blindness, we, like all the descendants of the Man and the Woman, can only *almost* see it, the place we really belong. There remains in our collective awareness a hazy sense of what should be and a clear conviction that this is not it. Our senses grow increasingly numb to true beauty, impatient with "received" wisdom, as our thoughts are taken more and more captive by tragic ignorance.

The earth and its children still languish and mourn. That is the hard, bad news.

It would have been no surprise if God had chosen to blot out the world as quickly as it became, to start over from scratch. But the good, true news is that God has never been able to brush us off, not entirely, though more than once since Eden He has wanted to do so. The Flood, even, was not water enough to get us off God's hands.

God made the world and gave it to us as a gift. We broke it as quickly and completely as children do a Christmas toy, but God determined to fix what was broken, both the world and us, but at first mostly from a distance. God chose a man and his sons—Noah and his heirs—to be the seeds of a new crop.

God delivered and constituted a people, Israel, sent laws and rituals, priests, prophets, and kings, that through them light might again shine in the world's darkness like new day. It was a re-creation, that the world itself might be blessed, the earth gradually a garden once more. But the many laws were disobeyed as quickly as Eden's, and the people soon disarrayed. Their kings and priests and prophets proved hard-hearted as the poor, dry earth where the holy people[3] lived, prickly as the thorns and broken as the world they were sent to redeem. As the fields grew more barren, the darkness grew deeper.

On the first Sunday of Advent I invite the children of our congregation down to the front of the sanctuary for the children's sermon, a liturgically suspect but customary element of our morning worship. When they arrive I have in my hand a butane lighter. Silently, once, twice, three times I pull the trigger. Blue and orange flame leaps from the tip. The kids say nothing, are transfixed by the sight, the flame.

"What have I just done?" I ask them. Little hands shoot into the air, polite eagerness. "You are making fire," one says. "That's what we use to light the altar candles," says another. "You're playing a game!" says an older child.

"It is fun," I say, "but it is not a game. Not really. I've said a prayer."

All look puzzled. "A *prayer*?" says one incredulously.

"Absolutely," I say. "When we light the candles on our altar, or pull the trigger on the lighter, or even strike a match . . . it is like a prayer. We are confessing—do you know that word? *Confessing? Confession?* We are admitting, confessing, that we are in the dark, like when you are in your house and there is a storm, thunder and lightning, and the lights go out, and you feel afraid. When it is really dark all of us get really scared. We don't know if we are alone or if someone is with us. If someone is with us, we are not sure whether they are our friends or not. And what we all wish, when that happens, is that the lights would come back on.

"Sometimes when we say we are 'in the dark,' we mean that we don't understand why things happen the way they do. We don't know why other people are the way they are; we don't even always know why we are like we are. We don't know why people are mean to each other and kill each other, why there is war and hunger and so much unhappiness.

"We light the candle," I say, "and it is like asking God to send us more light."

And we believe that, somehow and someway, God always answers that prayer.

Seven hundred years before the time of Jesus, the prophet Isaiah saw a vision, a vision we recall each Advent season:

> There shall come forth a shoot from the stump of Jesse,
>> and a branch shall grow out of his roots,
> And the Spirit of the LORD shall rest upon him.[4]

Isaiah's was a two-sided vision, really, a vision both of judgment and of grace. God is coming, will soon send a light so bright as to blind eyes too comfortable in the dark, a lamp that will illumine minds discontent in the long, deep shadows. God is coming: The promise and prospect is both judgment and mercy. Isaiah sees both at once, and that is precisely why we remember his prophecies each Advent season.

Like Isaiah's vision, the season of Advent—beginning the fourth Sunday before Christmas Day and ending Christmas Eve—proclaims both grace and judgment, mercy and indictment. It is grace, a joy and a celebration, that Jesus is coming to save us, that God loved the world so much—loved so much *the world*—that He sent His Son, that whoever believes in Him should not die but will live forever. But it is judgment too. It is an indictment that the world is indeed perishing, and Jesus must come lest we drown in the darkness. It is amazing that Jesus is near and terrifying to know that His presence portends not only life but also death, and not only for Him. All the instruments and idols and powers of darkness die with Him, the idolatries and darkness in ourselves as well, that light once again may shine forth as on the world's first day.

In his vision, Isaiah saw the end of old things and the beginning of new things, the death of what had seemed immortal—the kingdom of Israel and the throne of David—and the resurrection of what, long years after the coming destruction, would have seemed to be irretrievably lost.

But Isaiah saw something else, again when others could not. He knew that beyond the red was the green, that on the far side of the doom God was preparing an otherwise unimaginable redemption. After all was reduced to rubble and ash, when the cities were still smoldering and all of Israel's kings either dead or gone, Isaiah could see the Spirit of God moving across the face of the dark destruction, brooding over the ruined valleys and hills, caressing and coaxing and watering with His own tears that dry stump of Jesse till a shoot came forth, a surprising sprig from dead roots. The prophet proclaimed the coming of a King from the withered loins of long-ago David's long-dead father, foretold the arrival of a Son and wise ruler who would put things right again, who would build up the ancient ruins and strengthen the weak knees. On this Coming One the Spirit of the Lord would rest. The Spirit would give Him gifts too: wisdom and understanding and might, knowledge and compassion and fear of the Lord.

Isaiah described Him this way:

He shall not judge by mere appearances
    nor decide under the influence of spin,
but with righteousness he will vindicate the oppressed
    and advocate with equity for the meek of the earth.
His word will reorder the world
    and his life-giving breath will be the death of oppressors.[5]

For far too long there had been no justice, no truth, no peace. But, Isaiah proclaimed, a new King was coming.

Seven centuries before the angel appeared to a young woman of Nazareth, Isaiah saw the coming of One who for his own time, for his own people and circumstance, would be the very presence and power of God. Much, much later, after the virgin from Nazareth had conceived and given birth to a Son—and after that Son had grown up and become an itinerant rabbi, teaching and working miracles, after He had died and was raised to new life—those who loved Him and followed Him and preached His message would read Isaiah's prophecy and recognize the very face and work of their friend, Jesus. In *Him* judgment and mercy meet, "righteousness and peace . . . kiss each other,"[6] and by the power of the Holy Spirit a new people are born.

The promise of Advent is the wonderful, horrible promise of a new King, a new thing, a new way, and a new One sent to set things right. There are some who can smell it, the aroma of God's imminent justice, like the coming rain. Others smell only smoke. Many sense nothing at all, and not everyone will welcome God's reign when it arrives at last.

But the promise of Advent is that God is coming, nonetheless, sending One who is the heart of His own heart to be what the others He had sent were not: the very presence of God in the world, so that God's children might not be alone; the very light of God in the darkness, so that hearts and minds might be illumined; the very healing of God, so that the earth itself and all its people might be whole.

We embrace the darkness, but God knows we can no longer see, at least not clearly. We have all but forgotten Home and search, many times cluelessly, for that which we can no longer name. But in compassion God sends us a Shepherd, a Guide, and Guardian.

We are wounded, deny it as we will, and the life is pouring out of us. We finger the emptiness as we would a scar, bandage it with burlap, palliate it with various poison elixirs. We love that which will kill us, we hate that which might heal us, and we look for security, for comfort, in all the wrong places—such is our madness, the ancient chaos, the dark night of our soul's world. Into that very darkness God comes, God ever comes. God does not abandon us to our own self-destruction but sends light, speaks promise, gives new life.

Advent is the dark background to every portrait of Jesus. It confesses our present plight and proclaims the coming light. It does not engage in denial or optimism, escapism or opiates. Advent is, instead, the most "protestant" of seasons, protesting and militating for joy in spite of the grim sadness in us and in the world. It avows the deep brokenness of all things, the ruin of the world and its children, and hails the soon-healing of both. Advent admits to our fears and failure and invokes a hope to usurp and supplant them. It proclaims a coming redemption that, though we cannot see it whole, is even now on its way.

We confess we are in the dark. That is our side of the conversation in Advent. "Mercy and grace," God says again and again. "Peace and love." These are God's promises in the dark, God's signature gifts—illumination and hope for every lightless place. He knows we are dust, so He stoops once again to cradle us, to cradle grace for us, to breathe into us His own breath. He knows that we, like the world, are broken but there is healing in His wings.

Having loved us at the beginning, God will love us to the end. And endlessly in between, in every moment and maze, God calls to us, sings to us, invites us back into Eden, back into the very intimacies with God and each other for which we were made. Over and over God calls, waits, woos, beckons, encourages. Though we are all of us east of Eden—parted from God as far as the prodigal son was from his father, in a dark, far country of sin or indifference—God waits, looks, hopes, desires that all His children come back Home, to where there is food and song and reunion. Though we pretend to be content in the pigsty of our rebellions, below our protestations we writhe for Home as God's patient heart beats a cadence for our return. God comes to us that we might come back to Him: He makes and shows us the way.

God comes as near to us as He can in love, ever calls us to come the rest of the way to Him in faith. It is a long, hard journey on both ends, whether God's trek to us or ours to God.

Many years ago now, during a dark and extremely scary time in my life, when tears were my food both day and night, I found myself working second shift for just above minimum wage at a bookstore in Atlanta. I was the assistant manager, which meant I was the one to get in trouble if the cash drawer was short, the one who had to close and lock the doors.

As luck would have it—I guess it was luck—the sections of the store for which I was primarily responsible were "Religion," which comprised Christianity, Judaica, world religions, and the occult, and "Recovery," which included all the latest titles by Dr. Laura, Dr. Phil, Dr. Ruth, Deepak Chopra, Leo Buscaglia, Tony Robbins, and the like.

Many, many nights I saw people come into the store and, turning neither to the right nor to the left, head straight toward the big sign hanging from the ceiling that said "Self-Help," our best-selling section.

One December night—I remember it as if it were yesterday—I saw a young woman standing in the aisle, her heavy coat and scarf unable to hide that her shoulders were shaking as she quietly sobbed.

I was worried about her at once, my pastor's heart wanting to lend a pastor's ear and maybe a pastor's hand to her, whatever was the trouble. I approached her, at first as if to offer customer service: "Can I help you find something?"

She did not look up at first but said in a quavering voice, "I wish you could. I need to find *something*."

"You need help, then," I said after a moment.

Her throat clutched. "Yeah, I do. I need help."

"So do I," I said. "So do we all, and the poor dark world besides." That is when she turned and looked at me and I could see that her eyes were puffy, her skin streaked and blotched. She was a mess, and not just because her mascara wasn't waterproof. For the briefest of moments, I was not the assistant manager but her impromptu counselor. I pointed up to the big sign above us and whispered, "But the help we need, my friend, is beyond the self to provide."

I had to help another customer then, and when I looked back, the young woman was gone. I sometimes wonder whatever happened to her. One part of me thinks she is still there, our lady of perpetual desperation, still crying, still scanning the latest batch of self-help titles by the latest gaggle of self-help gurus, her shoulders still shaking and her makeup still streaked because there is no help there, no real healing, no lasting hope. She is a study in futility because she thinks she has to get help for herself, to make whatever little good might happen happen, build her best life now as God, if there is a God, helps only those who help themselves.

But another part of me thinks she took that little piece of advice, followed those simple directions, took a step toward Jesus and the Church, and there found what she could not find before, something bigger and better and beyond herself, a sprig growing from dry wood. A Savior who knows who we are and what we need and how to give it to us. In Him we find ways to understand the times, the moments and meanings of our lives, the first inklings of healing.

My prayer is that into the rough timbers of her life and circumstances holiness was born that night, that the presence of Christ came as light in her darkness. That likewise into our lives and the world's life, Christ may come.

Even so, come quickly, Lord Jesus.

Affirmation: Creation is good, then broken.

Confession: We too are broken.

Discipleship Task: To see the world and ourselves realistically and to wait, praying for the healing Jesus alone can bring.

Christmas [Middle English *Christemasse*, from Old English *Cristes mæsse*, literally, Christ's mass] **1:** a Christian feast on December 25 or among some Eastern Orthodox Christians on January 7 that commemorates the birth of Christ and is usually observed as a legal holiday

Chapter 2

God with Us

Christmas

In Jesus' birth... Christians believe two wonderful things happen. First, God takes the human life of Jesus into God's own eternal life, and in so doing, Jesus' people (the Jews), species (the human race), and history (the history of our whole planet and our whole universe) enter into — are taken up into — God's own life.... Second, as humanity (and all creation) enters into God through Jesus, God also enters Jesus' people, species, and history. And by entering all creation through Jesus, God's heart is forever bound to it in solidarity, faithfulness, loyalty, and commitment. God will never give up until all creation is healed.... Jesus saves by coming, by being born.

— Brian McLaren

This little babe so few days old, is come to rifle Satan's fold;
All hell doth at his presence quake, though he himself for
    cold do shake;
For in this weak unarm-ed wise, the gates of hell he will
    surprise;

With tears he fights and wins the field, his naked breast
     stands for a shield;
His battering shots are babish cries, his arrows looks of weep-
     ing eyes;
His martial ensigns Cold and Need, and feeble Flesh his
     warrior's steed.
His camp is pitch-ed in a stall, his bulwark but a broken wall;
The crib his trench, haystacks his stakes, of shepherds he his
     muster makes;
And thus, as sure his foe to wound, the angels' trumps alarum
     sound.
My soul, with Christ join thou in flight, stick to the tents
     that he hath dight.
Within his crib is surest ward, this little babe will be thy
     guard.
If thou wilt foil thy foes with joy, then flit not from this heav-
     enly boy.

— TWELFTH-CENTURY CAROL

Zechariah, the old and withered husband of childless Elizabeth, the elder cousin to unmarried Mary, was a priest, a righteous man, the Scripture says,[1] and full of the Holy Spirit, as was his wife. But his flesh was as dry as a wood plank. One day Zechariah was serving in the temple, perhaps for the first and only time in his long, priestly life, and while he did his sacred work, the angel Gabriel visited him, told him that he and Elizabeth were going to be parents.

Startled, Zechariah questioned the angel, "How can this be when I am ancient? Elizabeth and I have already forgotten the old tricks; how can we learn any new ones?"[2]

Gabriel was annoyed, and rightly so. After all, this was no ordinary announcement, and Gabriel no ordinary messenger. Besides, as a priest Zechariah should have remembered Israel's stories, how Sarah, Rachel, and Hannah were childless but all conceived in their old age because with God nothing is impossible. The very temple in which Zechariah stood bore witness through its stones and songs, its sacrifices and stories, that God comes as He wills, when and how He wills. But Zechariah was bedazzled, befuddled, and for a moment he forgot where he was, misplaced his stories, and doubted the angel's announcement (though not the angel's *reality*).

And so Gabriel summarily muted Zechariah for his impudence. The old priest would remain silent for the next nine months, with his faithless foot in his mouth. But his punishment would prove a blessing. He was able to ponder his next words carefully, choose them a bit more wisely. Sure enough, when he did finally speak again, it was the praise of God he uttered before he said another thing. Zechariah finally had it right.

We ourselves might do well with a season of silence, if only because we are sometimes so busy with our work, making our way in the world, that we do not hear the heavenly word should it come. "Do not be afraid," perhaps, or "Your prayer has been heard." We talk too much and hear too much—our ears so full of music or news or sports—to be able really to listen. There is so much noise in our world and in our lives. Partly because we have learned to fill every potentially silent moment with sound, we have become afraid of the silence. And perhaps, in fact, we are. There is so much movement in our world and in our lives. Partly because we have learned to fill every waking moment with activity, we have become afraid of the stillness. And perhaps, in fact, we are. But without stilling ourselves, without taking time to listen, we will never hear the still, small voice of God.

If the old priest was silenced because he heard God's promises and did not trust them, we may need silencing *to* hear them.

In the sixth month of Zechariah's silence and Elizabeth's pregnancy, a virgin named Mary espoused to a tradesman named Joseph, living in Nazareth, had a similar visitation.[3] She was at home, presumably, when Gabriel appeared to her and announced that she would conceive and bear a Son. It was the same message, basically, that Gabriel had delivered to Zechariah. But if his incredulity was surprising, hers was not.

"How can this be, since I am so young?"

This time Gabriel answered gently: "The Holy Spirit will come upon you, will overshadow you, will conceive holiness in you, and you shall bear in your womb and deliver to this earth a savior."[4] From Gabriel's lips to Mary's ear. Her response rose from deep within her: "Let it be to me according to your word." By God's own initiative the Word is made with Mary's flesh. Mary was but the first of the *theotokoi*.[5] She cradled the Christ in her womb, of course, but all those who do the will of God, who answer the call to discipleship and love God's appearing,[6] are not only Jesus' friends and followers, His brothers and sisters, but also His *mother*.[7] Those who hear the command of God and do it, who bring good news to the poor and proclaim release to the captives, who announce sight for the blind and freedom for the oppressed, who preach the Lord's favor[8] — all of them gestate God's will, give birth to God's Word and purposes

God-bearer

in the world. The Holy Spirit comes, overshadows, and holiness is born. Mary birthed Jesus once; His disciples birth Him over and over and over again.

Gabriel did not silence Mary as he did Zechariah but instead gave her voice to sing a song of faith, one she sang a short time later in the home of her cousin Elizabeth—the *Magnificat*:

My soul magnifies the Lord,
and my spirit rejoices in God my Savior,
for he has regarded the low estate of his handmaiden.
For behold, henceforth all generations will call me blessed;
for he who is mighty has done great things for me,
and holy is his name.[9]

Compare the two moments: Gabriel's visit to the old priest and his visit to the young virgin six months later. The stories are so similar, yet so very different. Mary (and her cousin Elizabeth) sang praise to God earlier and more faithfully. Zechariah eventually did as well, but only after many silent nights.

When Mary visited Elizabeth, Zechariah could not discuss with them the angel, the visitations, and the incredible news, at least not in words. But his eyes twinkled with tears, shimmered like stars in the night sky. He knew something amazing, even if for the moment he could not talk about it.

It was Mary and Elizabeth who did all the talking, but not as we might expect expectant mothers to do. They did not talk about diets and exercise, how their feet were swelling, or how their backs already hurt.

Instead of lamenting what their unborn children were doing to them, already making day-to-day life miserable, they rejoiced in what God was about to do in the world through their children. Soon the "haves" would be the "have-nots" while the "have-nots" would have it all—the favor and blessing and mercy of God. The swollen, prideful kings would soon be withered, humiliated. The powerful who had gotten rich at the expense of the poor would be trading places with the outcast and the downtrodden. The outcasts would revel in a prosperity of God's own making.

Mary and Elizabeth knew, *knew*, that their sons were swords in the hands of God, cutting and cleaving and making straight, bringing down and building up, straightening and leveling. Soon the lowly would lift their voices in praise and thanksgiving, just as this barren, old woman and her young virgin cousin were doing: talking and singing, offering God and each other mystified thanks and adulation.

The highest praise is not imitation but amazed interrogation.

"How can this be," Elizabeth asked in wonder, "that the mother of my Savior would come to me?"[10]

"How can this be," the blessed virgin Mary asked innocently, "that the mighty arm of God has been revealed and it is the arm of a newborn? That all the purposes and power of God are enfleshed in my flesh? That the Light of the World is gestating in the darkness of my womb?"[11]

"How can this be?" Surely Joseph asked it too, as dumbfounded as Zechariah when he had asked the question of Gabriel. It was of Mary and God that Joseph asked the question, whether in rage or despair or both.

We do not know much about Joseph and are the poorer for it. There are apocryphal stories about him, most of them fanciful, funny, and completely unreliable.[12] The skinny: He was an old man, over ninety, when he was chosen by lot to be the guardian as much as the husband of Mary.

Mary's mother, Anna, conceived Mary in her old age and dedicated her daughter to God's service.[13] Anna brought Mary to the temple when Mary was twelve, at about the same time Joseph—a priest and father of six grown children—was left a widower at age eighty-nine. Two years later, when Mary was fourteen, the priests drew straws to see who would be caretaker for Mary, and Joseph found himself married to the young virgin. He was mostly beyond suspicion when her pregnancy was at last revealed and soon he moved this, his second family, to Nazareth where he lived another twenty years, dying at the age of 111.

To some early believers, this age disparity seemed a nice if indirect proof not only of Jesus' virginal conception but also of Mary's perpetual virginity.[14] It also helps explain why we never again hear of Joseph after the trip to the temple when Jesus was twelve and Joseph was, by my calculations, 103.

I don't much believe any of that, though.

I am more inclined to think of Mary and Joseph's relationship as typical, their love genuine, their plans more or less normal, and their future hopeful (if not terribly promising, what with Joseph a carpenter in a rocky land in the midst of Roman occupation). But every couple in young love sees the future as a cup brimming with promise, and the two must have talked about the home they planned to make, the draperies and dishes. Surely they talked about children too, how many they hoped to have and when. Everything, it seems, was going along as planned when . . .

"Joseph," Mary said quietly, "I am going to have a baby."

How he had wanted to hear those words, but not now, not like this. And now, whenever he heard them again, from whomever's lips, they would be a knife to his heart. If Joseph was human, even if he believed, he also doubted. Even if he hoped, he also despaired—for many reasons, not least that although Mary was his wife she was not carrying his child, not really.

He was afraid too. Afraid that what Mary told him was not true, and perhaps even more afraid that it was. He was angry and scared by turns, happy and sad, ready to put her away and eager to keep her close. He tried to hold on, was ready to let go, and did not know what to think or do. Finally he decided to divorce her, cancel their agreement, but quietly, mercifully—he did not want a scandal for her, did not want her accused of adultery and banished, or worse. It was only then, *after* he had made a gracious decision, that Joseph received an angelic visitation of his own, his own divine confirmation that it was all of it true. "Let it be to *me* according to your will," he might have prayed, and known peace.

Did he? Really? Ever? Do we believe because of our dreams or dream because of belief? The poet W. H. Auden maintains that Joseph was the first Christian: He decided to believe the news of the Incarnation and order his life accordingly, all without proof. He lived *as if* it was true, that his faith would become sight, his hope knowledge,[15] the first of many to do so.

The trajectory of discipleship seems to be this: We live faithfully until by grace we have faith. We hear the call, the announcement, the summons. God's call moves us one way or the other, shuffles our feet or opens our hands. By grace that call softens our heart, its final destination, and then we live faithfully because we have faith.

We travel on our way, living our lives *as if,* living in light of what ought to be true, even though we cannot be absolutely sure on this side of death that it is. We trace our steps by the hope of something beyond the path we see, beyond the directions we hear, acknowledging if we dare that we may be fools to do so. Somehow, though, we find the strength to keep answering, to keep moving, to keep making space for God to appear. We set our sights by what "cannot be seen," as Paul fashioned it, for "what can be seen is temporary, but what cannot be seen is eternal."[16] We keep going, believing and not, hoping and despairing, trusting that what we have heard—the call to faithfulness, even if we have heard it in our dreams—is the truest of all true things, the truth itself below all appearance.

And so the Holy Family—Mary, Joseph, and the unborn Savior—made their uncomfortable way, each of them bearing a heavy burden and all of them together a picture, a parable of our own pilgrim journeys till the Son of God be revealed at last. That day is near. God's will will be done. Redemption draweth nigh, but until it arrives, there is night.

In those days Caesar said that everyone had to travel to his or her ancestral home to be counted, to be taxed.[17] Even pregnant young women and perplexed young men had to hit the road. It is a long way from Nazareth to Bethlehem. A long way from God's heart to Mary's womb. A long way from Heaven to earth.

They came to Bethlehem, Mary and Joseph, she on a donkey and Jesus in her womb. Joseph led them both, being led himself. Each of them, in his or her own way, was in the dark about what lay ahead. Whether they were ready for all of it, or for any of it, when the time was right, the baby was born. And Joseph named Him Jesus.[18]

Jesus. A name that translates, "Lord, save us."

When Joseph named the baby Jesus, it was a prayer for himself and the world. Mary's was the first womb, but the world itself, all its times and peoples, is where God would swaddle the Divine. Jesus was born in the caves outside Bethlehem, for the sake of all who walk or sleep or are buried in the darkness. God so loved the world, but we sometimes forget.

Christmas, as we often observe it, blinds us to anything but Christmas itself. Its properties are those of an icon—a portal, written so as to channel the blessing and grace of God into the world. It is a window, opened to grant our prayers access to God. By grace we are granted, if we will, to see through the celebration itself to God's love of the world. "Glory to God in the highest and on earth, peace" is not a clichéd refrain for the children's angel chorus on pageant night but the full measure of God's will for the world and its children. Jesus is born to save the world, comes as healer for all His wounded children.

Each year on December 21, still on Advent's dark highway but almost in sight of Bethlehem's lights, I schedule a service called The Longest Night. The service, following Ann Weems, is for "those who weep and those who weep with those who weep."[19] The sanctuary lights are dimmed and the room illumined mostly by candles. There is barely enough light to read the dark Scriptures, sing the bleak, midwinter hymns, and remember all those for whom the Christmas season is unsparing and brutal. There is deep grief among some of the worshipers on account of various separations from loved ones. There are other weights too, other lonelinesses and sadnesses, weights on the hearts and feet of those who are dragging themselves through the festivities.

We keep moving through the season with the crowds, of course, one foot in front of the other—after all, what choice is there? But the star is not visible to some eyes, the angels do not sing in every ear. We tramp along as best we can, wanting to believe, or remembering belief, hoping against hope to believe again that Christ is at the end of the journey and therefore with us on the way.

During our prayers we remember the dead, and not just our own. We remember the struggling, the doubting, the hopeless and imprisoned. Those with withered hearts remember the man with the withered hand, how Jesus told him, there in the middle of the synagogue crowd, to reveal what he had long tried to keep hidden from everyone . . . and how healing came. Just then. As he confessed his shame. We too stretch out our wounded selves to Jesus.

One year a dear woman stood to tell us with cracking voice of her son who was addicted to so very many things, so very, very lost. She told us how she and her husband had lived with the shame of their son's plight, the guilt that they had done something wrong, and how they were crushed under the burden of his brokenness. The marriage was strained, they had little to say to each other or anyone else, so withered were their spirits, each of them defending what they needed to confess, hiding what they needed to share, grieving and angry in their own way, and unable to find a place or way to lay any of it down. Until that night. She stretched her wounded heart to Jesus, and she and her husband went to the altar to light a candle for their poor son, for his ex-wife and children—a prayer for all of them.

Suddenly, the room moved. Everyone attending the service stood and moved to the front to join them, to touch them, to hug and cry with them, to tell them of their love. On the heels of lonely confession came intimacy, as in our sanctuary, dark as the Bethlehem cave, there came light.

We gather each year to pray, to leave our fears and shame at the twinkling altar, hoping against hope that the Light shining in darkness will shine into our own hearts and lives, and the world as well. We sing:

O Little Town of Bethlehem, how still we see thee lie,
Above thy deep and dreamless sleep the silent stars go by.
Yet in thy dark streets shineth, the everlasting light.
The hopes and fears of all the years are met in thee tonight.
For Christ is born of Mary . . .

Christ is born of Mary. That is the hope. That too is the fear. That is the truth.

The darkness of Mary's womb cradled a Savior who will be a light to all people. The dark road to Bethlehem, a parable of our own dark roads, found its way. The overcrowded town, itself a parable of our overcrowded lives, hosted the Baby.

Advent is not just the story of Mary's pregnancy, but also of Elizabeth's and indeed the world's. The whole creation groans as if in labor pains[20] until all that God has promised is delivered. Until then, we make our uncomfortable way forward, remembering the stories and letting what we hear find its way to our heart. "Let it be to all of us according to Your Word, whatever that word may be." We hope and despair by turns that new life is possible on the other side of the darkness and pain, but we proclaim that God's promise is good, that the Promised One is coming.

But "how can anything good come from Nazareth?"[21] How indeed can anything good come *to* Narareth, or *to* Bethlehem, to the world, or even to our own lives? The answer, which is the root of the Story, is at once long-familiar and remains a surprise: grace, God's inestimable mercy, His self-prompted initiative.

God determined to intervene in our helplessness, to stab the darkness, to come to our aid. Though He is King of the universe, He would not be separated from His unfortunate people but came to take His place among and with them. Though high and lifted up, where He might have remained impassive to the weary misery of His children, having heard their cries, He condescended instead. He emptied Himself to fill the valleys, leveled the mountains with a cross, proved His power by humility and suffering and service. As it was in the beginning is now and ever shall be: God comes. Jesus is born.

Someone fashioned Bethlehem's manger, rough and splintery and uneven as its boards might have been. The laborer did not know the full meaning of the work he did, what grace the manger might come to hold. He opened a crack, shaped a place, divided the air, and made a space so that a living thing of its own accord might draw near, whether sheep or cows, shepherds or Wise Men, even the Lamb who is the Christ.

The Bethlehem worker made a trough, but it was up to God to crib salvation within. Still, Jesus could have not been swaddled precisely *there* had the laborer not sawed and hammered, splintered his fingers and bashed his thumbs, to make something to hold *something*.

We sometimes see light in the cracks of our lives. God's light seeps through our broken places. Our prayers may open a space for God to come, but it is left to God *to* come, to bring holiness to us, to note our hammering attentions and answer our rasping saws.

So we keep at it: saying our prayers, making a space, digging a cave should God decide to visit. There is no guarantee, of course. The prayer itself may prove the answer to our praying, which is to say that our work does not guarantee the arrival of righteousness. God is not on call. God, rather, does the calling and shows up where and when He will.

Still, what choice is there? We do as we have been instructed. We pray. We clothe the naked. We visit the prisons or feed the hungry, and who knows? Perhaps one Christmas Eve as we are in the local soup kitchen ladling the steaming broth, the eyes of a stranger will look up to us, and, as if through a plume of incense, we will see God come as one of the least of these.

Through the dark and broken places—that is where the light most often seeps. The cave that Bethlehem night was what it was, a hole in the hillside, an emptiness more than a presence, and the manger, rough-hewn at best. The house of our souls, as Augustine rightly saw, is no more than clapboard and emptiness. Our world is a hovel, one way or the other, but God comes. Bidden or unbidden, *vocare atque non vocare*—in spite of all, holiness gets born.

Somewhere. Sometime. Then in Bethlehem, now among us.

Not always where we would think to look for it, but always where we will find it, if we have the eyes to see.

When we least expect it.

When we most need it.

Sometimes in the mangers we have readied for Him, and sometimes in a space we have built for something else entirely.

God's grace, our work: Both play a part, but the phrases are not equally weighted. The latter depends wholly on the first, is the gist of our hopes and our prayers. We do our work, yes, but all the work we do is barest preparation. Holiness appears of its own accord.

Jesus arrives when the "days are accomplished." When the time is right, He comes. His holiness sanctifies the manger of our lives, His birth fills the dark caves of our world with light. Joy to the *world*. The Lord is come.

But not everyone is happy about it.

On December 26, the second day of Christmas, when our true love would give us what in Jesus' day was a temple sacrifice especially prescribed for the poor—two turtledoves—we remember and celebrate the martyrdom, the sacrifice, of Stephen. The Feast of Stephen, known to many only through the carol "Good King Wenceslas," is a solemn moment in the Church year. In it we recall the life and faithful death of the first disciple to die for *being* a disciple. It is a stark reminder that our faith is a matter of life and death. Jesus is a constant threat to the powers that be; following Him puts us at dangerous odds with the same sorts of folk who killed Him.

But Stephen's life and martyrdom shine like a star in the night, like the Bethlehem star, guiding the wise past the fear of death and all the way to the place where Jesus is. "I see the Son of Man, standing [standing, we suppose, so as to welcome Stephen home] on the right hand of the Father," Stephen said. His last words were, "Lord, do not hold this sin against them,"[22] a prayer remarkable not only for its generosity but also because it sounds so very much like Jesus' last words, some of them.[23]

Jesus' disciples are those who would die like Him, with faith and forgiveness on their lips. They are those who would live like Jesus too, who are determined to speak as Jesus spoke. Christians are those who can boast that they have never said or done anything original.

On December 28, the day of "four calling birds," we celebrate the Feast of the Holy Innocents, those children who gave their lives for Jesus so that He could give His life for others. The terrible tale is told in three verses of Matthew (2:16-18), as if to indicate that the evangelist himself barely had the stomach to tell it at all, how Herod in a rage had all the children in and around Bethlehem murdered. The Magi, so foolish for all their wisdom, visited the unstable king and told him they had seen a star, the herald of a new ruler for Israel. The king, fearful for all his power, sent his armies against the village's two-and-under toddlers. Their campaign succeeded with grim efficiency, but Herod's plan failed. Jesus, the newborn King, escaped. Many other children did not. These Holy Innocents cry out year by year that the message of Christmas is not just a sentimental pageant for bathrobed shepherds in handtowel headdresses, but a dread drama with dirges as well as carols accompanying.

"The Word became flesh and dwelt among us," John says.[24] If for Mary and Stephen and the Innocents that meant pain and blood and tears, for the powers and rulers of this world it means death in favor of God's new life.

Christ first dwelt among us in the unlit darkness of a Bethlehem cave, the limb-numbing cold of a Bethlehem night, there among smelly animals and all the smelly things stabled animals do. It was not a pristine moment, though the Hallmark cards would like us to think otherwise. There would be few pristine moments to follow. At the beginning and again at the end there was the tearing of skin, the pouring of blood, and screams of pain. The Word taking on Mary's flesh was a dangerous and untidy business. Following Jesus proves just as dangerous, just as untidy.

That some can welcome the Holy Family or the Holy One only sentimentally while others cannot welcome them at all should come as no surprise. Jesus' arrival makes a difference, creates a divide, breaks things in two: history, religions, hearts. There is joy but there is also sadness. There is life but there is also death. There is mercy but there is at the same time judgment, each attending the other. There is separation, as at Creation, and there is reconciliation for the making and remaking of the world. There is blood and pain and sometimes the rending of flesh, but all for the healing and restoration of the nations.

The nations will be healed, the world restored. The zeal of the Lord of hosts will do this, for

> a child has been born for us,
>   a son given to us;
> authority rests upon his shoulders;
>   and he is named
> Wonderful counselor, Mighty God,
>   Everlasting Father, Prince of Peace.
> His authority shall grow continually,
>   and there shall be endless peace . . .
>   from this time onward and forevermore.[25]

God does not retreat from our calamity. God does not abandon us to our self-destruction or leave us as food for the darkness. God comes, and will again. For amazingly, incredulously, God so loved the world.

Affirmation: Jesus' birth is proof that God loves the broken world.

Confession: We doubt/ignore/reject God's love for the world.

Discipleship Task: To celebrate God's love for the world by making space in our lives to receive Jesus in all the ways He comes to us.

PART TWO

OUR FAITHFUL RESPONSE

Epiphany [Middle English *epiphanie*, from Anglo-French, from Late Latin *epiphania*, from Late Greek, plural, probably alteration of Greek *epiphaneia* appearance, manifestation, from *epiphainein* to manifest, from *epi-* + *phainein* to show] **1:** capitalized: January 6 observed as a church festival in commemoration of the coming of the Magi as the first manifestation of Christ to the Gentiles or in the Eastern Church in commemoration of the baptism of Christ **2:** an appearance or manifestation especially of a divine being **3a** (1): a usually sudden manifestation or perception of the essential nature or meaning of something

Chapter 3

From an Exclusive to an Inclusive Faith

Epiphany

In saying, "He ascended," what does it mean but that he had also descended into the lower parts of the earth? He who descended is he who also ascended far above all the heavens, that he might fill all things.

— Ephesians 4:9-10

Jesus loves the little children, all the children of the world:
Red and yellow, black and white, they are precious in his
  sight.
Jesus loves the little children of the world.

— anonymous

The hope of all who seek him, the help of all who find . . .
— Alfred H. Ackley, 1933

All parents know that sooner or later the time will come when their children will ask, "Where did I come from?" Some parents I have known, hoping to treat their little ones as adults, answer the questions biologically. They may say, "You came from your mother's belly," or "womb," even, and so proceed to give their children the cellular facts as best they can.

Other parents answer the question as they themselves might have been answered, more mythologically. "The stork brought you," or some such. Each answer works in its own way, if only because it postpones further discussion to a later season, and many times that is what parents want. But in many other ways, neither answer works and does not tell what inquiring children most want to know. At least that is how a friend assessed the situation as she described the moment when her little girl asked, "Mommy, where was I before I was born?" My friend, in a moment of high inspiration, answered spiritually. Tears spilled as she said, "In the heart of God, honey. Before we knew you, you were in the heart of God. And we are so glad God gave you to us." Several months later, she said, they talked biology, but those facts were less important to her child than the truth, which is that she was a gift of God's heart, a sign of God's love.

My friend Ron says that the best of these kinds of conversations occur when the child is adopted, for that is when parents might well answer theologically. When his son Chris asked the perennial question—he was observant enough to see he didn't look a thing like Ron or Ron's wife, Louise, and he had been old enough when he joined their household to have some disparate memories—Ron said, "We chose you, Chris. We had always wanted a son and God made it possible for us to have you. You were a gift."[1]

Other questions followed: "Who is my real mother? Did she not want me? Is something wrong with me that she gave me away?" And yet, Ron said, as hard as those questions were — and there was nothing easy about them — Chris seemed more or less content with the sharp edges of his story because he really did believe it when Ron said, "We chose you. We adopted you. We wanted you to be a part of our family."

Epiphany offers the wondering world similar loving testimony, tells us of God's plan from the beginning of the world to its end: to choose all of us, to unite all of fractured humanity into one family, one people.[2] Sadly, despite angelic announcements and prophetic pronouncements — indications now and then of God's ultimate will and purposes — many of God's children possess ears too deaf to hear, hearts too hard to trust all that has been spoken by God and the prophets. The fullness of God's gracious intent has often been muted, and even now among some it lies buried beneath landslides of tribalism, pride, and misunderstanding.

When God first spoke to Abram, God said, "I will make of you a great nation, and I will bless you, and make your name great, so that you will be a blessing. . . . And in you all the families of the earth shall be blessed."[3] Many times and places, among many of God's peoples, that first cluster of God's promises was remembered and trumpeted while the second cluster was minimized, if not ignored, qualified, roped off with many requirements.

For some generations of Abraham's heirs (and perhaps for some in *every* generation), to be "chosen" suggested special privilege and advantage. It is understandable. They had been entrusted with the land, the Law, and the temple. God had called *them*, not others, and had made them a distinct people, set apart for the task of knowing and doing God's will. If they had been given a unique identity and work, no wonder many came to believe that they also had an exclusive and excluding relationship to God and God's will. God's requirements for them became their prerequisites for everyone else, and no outsider might imagine they could have audience with *their* God—or even come very near the temple—without a painful conversion to Judaism. And woe be to the born-Jew who intermarried or otherwise mingled with outsiders.[4]

Not everyone felt this way, of course. Many of the prophets reminded the Israelites that God's grace was for all people, that they were but the channels of that grace, that humility was their posture and service their means of bringing God's blessing into the world.

All people were invited to the mountain to worship,[5] a sign of God's borderless and everlasting peace. But even then, like now, not everyone wanted to hear that inclusive word. Some imagined God as their own possession, His blessing their particular right, and prosperity their inevitable destiny.

So it is no surprise that even such a prophet as Jonah, called to preach in Nineveh in the east, set sail for the west. God's insistent mercy was stronger than Jonah's dissent, however, and if in the darkness of the fish's belly Jonah did not exactly see the light, when the fish coughed him up on the shore and God told him, once again, to go preach in Nineveh, he did. Unenthusiastically, to be sure, begrudging both the city's repentance and God's pardon. But Jonah proves a prophet of God's will in spite of himself, that

God loves not only repentant Ninevites but even defiant Israelites. God's mercy is God's to give, and over and over He gives it to all His children.[6]

What God showed Jonah, others had already seen. Long before Jonah had hair, Isaiah called out that God would soon provide a "light to the nations" so that salvation might reach the ends of the earth.[7] The prophet foresaw a time when God's servant would call to nations He did not know, that untold nations would in turn run to Him.[8]

From the heart of God through the mouths of the prophets, the Word comes to our ears. From the foundations of the world to the skies over the Judean countryside, the Light comes to our eyes. From the manger in Bethlehem to all who see and follow the star—there is light, there is unveiling, there is enlightening. We discover divine treasure long-hidden in the fields of time, good news for all people, to the Gentiles as well as the Jews, to the Jews no less than to the Gentiles.

Epiphany, both the day (January 6) and the weeks-long season (until Ash Wednesday and the beginning of Lent), has been celebrated since at least the fourth century. It reminds us that God's ultimate purpose is to bring all of His children into the sphere of His mercy and blessing—to unite all things in Christ, things in Heaven and things on earth. God's is a radical hospitality; His inclusions obliterate every exclusion.

The season's message is prophetic, as it warns those who dare narrow the scope of God's redeeming love, who would circumscribe grace with a tight line of nation or tradition, language or race—and God's disciples not least. The message is pastoral too, for those who, for one reason or the other, have felt on the other side of erstwhile lines.

While the full scope of God's plan, along with the identity of the One who will accomplish it,[9] has been mostly hidden until now, Epiphany unveils, proclaims, celebrates God's gift to all people. No surprise then that the first and primary narrative for Epiphany is Matthew's story of the Magi. Their arrival is celebrated on January 6, the day after the Twelfth Day of Christmas, the morning after the Twelfth Night. As God comes to the world in Jesus, the world comes to Jesus in the Magi. Gentiles bring gifts to the Jew; Jews bring the gift of Christ to the Gentiles.

Visitors from the East come when Jesus is still in diapers, Wise Men who had foolishly announced to the reigning king, the madman Herod, that a baby had been born to usurp his throne. Tradition tells us, based mostly on the number of gifts they brought, that there were three Wise Men. Later tradition even assigned them names: Caspar, Melchior, and Balthazzar. They are almost an afterthought, set dressing, the final act of the children's annual Christmas pageant. Because the play is already running long and the toddler-angels are getting fidgety and reaching for the chrismons, we rush the Wise Men to the manger's side, a regal denouement to the drama. The last to arrive, they are first to leave again. And in most every church's Nativity scene, there are the Wise Men standing next to the shepherds and gazing down on the newborn baby Jesus.

But the Magi most likely arrived much later, as much as two years after Jesus' birth, given Herod's infanticidal decree. Their coming, their worship, is not a sentimental afterthought at all, but the first dramatic notes sounded in a new movement of Jesus' life and God's purposes. These Gentile Magi are a long way from where they might ever have imagined themselves to be, on a strange mission to bring gifts to they know not whom, a young stranger, a

Hebrew male child, a great King. The gold, frankincense, and myrrh are signs both of their fealty and their faith in a reality beyond any conventional, political, or palatial wisdom.

They followed the star, a bright ball of grace in the West—a hole punched in the night—and there for all the world to see, but not everyone did and even those who noticed, most of them, did not recognize its significance or move their feet to its song. Its appearance was cryptic, an astrometric rune to be translated, hidden in plain sight from the oblivious or inattentive.

If the star was pure grace, the Magi's travel is sheer faith—hard work with a dash of lunacy thrown in. Like Israel in the wilderness long generations before, the Magi pilgrim in search of what, until they find it, is only a promise.

Their worship is the dawn of a new age, foreshadowing the Day when there will be no shadows at all, no veils covering the eyes or ears of God's children, when all peoples will come to the mountain of God to feast and rejoice and sing praise.

The Wise Men came seeking Jesus, and it is a parable. He came to His own—His own world, His own people—and though many despised and rejected Him, there were and remain many who saw Him, full of grace and truth, Jews and Gentiles alike. His natal star, like a flashlight in the hand of God, led the Magi up the dark and rocky path till it came to where the Child lay and glittered their believing eyes. The wise still come as testimony that He is the only hope for the dark, sad world, the King of the Jews and the Savior of the world.

The foolish Wise Men followed a star, and like the frightened shepherds who saw the glory of the Lord shining all around them, they all of them somehow found their way to the One who would prove light in the darkness, peace in the chaos, oasis in the wilderness, and company along the way. We too, though just as foolish and frightened, may find that He is the help of all who seek Him, the hope of all who find.

The Gentile sages fulfill Isaiah's prophecy in their coming and thereby raise the curtain on a new season in the Christian year—Epiphany. The name is a transliteration of a Greek word whose definition is "unveiling," and it tells the story of how the one born King of the Jews is also Savior of the world. For God so loved *the world* He sent Jesus.

The Church exists to reiterate that message, full as it is of grace and comfort and also of prophetic warning and challenge to the powers and principalities of this world. The Magi, kings of the earth, came to Jesus. This is the first story of Epiphany. The stories that follow tell of Jesus going into the world proclaiming the kingdom of God, good news for all who will welcome it, of God's coming reign over all the earth.

Jesus told parables.

We do not read very far in the New Testament before we are confronted with the stories Jesus told, the riddles and vignettes—a man had two sons; a sower went out to sow; a woman misplaced a coin; a shepherd lost a sheep. "With many such parables [Jesus] spoke the word," Mark tells us. He goes on to say that Jesus "did not speak to them except in parables, but he explained everything in private to his disciples."[10]

Explanation was sometimes necessary, and most always welcome, if only because what Jesus meant, what He was saying, was not always obvious.

"What shepherd, having one hundred sheep, if he loses one, does not leave the ninety-nine in the wilderness and go seeking the one that is lost?"[11] Well, *no* shepherd does that, frankly. Most shepherds would consider a 1 percent loss acceptable and, especially in savage environs, would work to protect the others. But not this Shepherd. He leaves His flock alone, in the wilds, where there are lions and tigers and bears, oh my—and goes after one sheep. ONE! The Good Shepherd will not willingly suffer the loss of any of those entrusted to Him, though it puts both His followers and Himself at some risk to seek and to save the lost sheep.

The woman who misplaces the coin, once she finds it, spends more on the party than she had lost to begin with.[12] The foolish sower slings seed everywhere and thereby proves the wisdom of God.[13] The father, whose younger son has wished him dead, welcomes him back with festival and song, much to the chagrin of his older son who has been faithful all along.[14]

Jesus spun His tales, and some had the ears to hear and eyes to see, but some did not. As it was in the beginning is now and ever shall be. Even those who wanted to understand didn't. Don't. The kingdom of God is like new wine,[15] like treasure buried in a field.[16] It is like a mustard seed,[17] or yeast in three measures of flour.[18] It is like birth,[19] like death,[20] like the wind.[21] Jesus told parables, and a scholar I used to know would say that they are like a good joke—if you get it, you really get it, it opens your eyes; and if you don't get it, you feel blinder, deafer, dumber, than you already know yourself to be.

Parables tell the truth, all the truth, but they tell it "slant," as Emily Dickinson wrote.[22] The kingdom of God is like a bush, with lots of different birds singing lots of different songs.[23] It is like a fig tree.[24] It is like a vineyard.[25] The parables "dazzle us gradually" so that we are not blinded as with bolts of lightning rending our darkness. No, the surprise of truth comes more like fingers of dawn at the far edge of our incomprehension, as a promise of incremental understanding. We are gradually enabled, bit by bit, to see. A parable is like the sunrise for those who are awake and looking.

Jesus told parables. He also *was* a parable in His life and ministry, in the things He did and the things that happened around Him. For those with eyes to see, it was all of it a kind of slant truth-telling. God's grace was not bound by time, Jesus said, and proved as much when He healed on the Sabbath. Neither was God's regard limited to some. Jesus healed *women* on the Sabbath, *taught* women the Law. He talked to a *Samaritan* woman in public and made a Samaritan man the hero of His most famous story. Jesus broke the conventional taboos for the sake of life and healing and the kingdom.

The religious leaders were increasingly, perpetually furious and determined to stop Him, to put Him to death if need be. But if Jesus did His work in public—"Stretch out your withered hand for all to see," He said to the man in the synagogue[26]—Jesus' opponents did their work in secret, kept their withered hearts hidden and safe from His healing touch.

One time, Jesus touched a leper who wanted healing.[27] He had been teaching the night before in Capernaum, at the home of Simon and Andrew. Earlier that day Jesus had healed Simon's mother-in-law, and word spread so quickly that at sundown—the start of a new day—just about the whole town came bringing their sick and their selves in hopes Jesus would heal them too. And He did. But the next morning, while it was still a long time before daylight, Jesus got up and went to a lonely place to pray. As He sought the Father, the disciples hunted for the Son, and after they found Him, they said, "We have to go back and do that again." Jesus said, "We have to go on ahead, so that I can preach in the next towns, for *that* is what I came to do."[28]

And that is what He was doing when the leper came to Him and said, "If you choose, you can make me clean." Our Bibles say that Jesus was moved with compassion when He saw the young man, that He chose on the basis of that compassion to heal him.[29] But there is a strong tradition that Jesus' first reaction was not compassion but anger.[30] If He healed the man, Jesus Himself would be unclean, unable to enter the towns to preach, unable to do what He had set out to do. The leper was an interruption, but Jesus chose to heal him *anyway*. For Jesus to heal this unfortunate man was to sacrifice His own desire.

The story is a parable, an example of how Jesus altered His itinerary, did something else, spent Himself in a new way for the sake of the one who asked Him. He cast His lot with outsiders, called many of His disciples from the fringe. Jesus came to His own, over and over again, choosing them, taking His righteous place even among the unrighteous.

Jesus came to the Jordan River to be baptized by His cousin John. The Baptizer had set up prophetic shop far away from what he considered the corrupted precincts of Jerusalem and its temple, its maculate priests and practices.[31] John took his place down by the riverside and Jesus came there too, stood shoulder-to-shoulder with the riffraff and sinners, the vipers and snakes John routinely excoriated. All of these desired water baptism as a sign of repentance, but what they really needed, John said, was fire baptism and real repentance, gifts neither he nor the river could give. They needed a bathing deeper than Jordan's reach, a subcutaneous watering to let these barren and withered "trees"[32] bring forth worthy fruit. And when Jesus waded into the Jordan to be baptized, John tried to prevent Him, saying, "It is I who should be baptized by you, and yet do you come to me?"

Yes. And yes. John, like the rest of them, needed the gift that only Jesus could give. So Jesus did, in fact, come to him.

"Yes," Jesus said, "I do come to you." Jesus shows Himself Messiah and Savior, Son of Man and Son of God as He, who needed neither baptism nor repentance, comes to those who need both. He came to the Jordan that day, and He comes even today, to fonts and baptisteries and riversides, because He is not afraid to be known by the company He keeps, and also because He keeps company with God. Jesus came to the Jordan to be baptized by John, and John would have prevented Him, but Jesus said to His cousin, "Let it be so now [and] . . . in this way to fulfill all righteousness."[33]

Righteousness was all of them taking their proper places: John in the water, the crowds by the riverside, and Jesus with the crowds — not above them, lording Himself over the citizens of His kingdom, but beside them, among them, shoulder-to-shoulder and cross-to-cross. Though the people knew not who was in their midst, still He loved them and served them. He knew, if they did not, that they would soon reject Him, most of them, but still He came to the Jordan, took His righteous place for and with the unrighteous. Immanuel, doing God's will and fulfilling His own purpose by taking His dusty place, His damp with water or blood place, lowered there by another's hands into the river or the tomb.

As He came out of the water, there was a dove, but not everyone saw it. There was a voice, but not everyone heard it or understood. Jesus saw, and He knew. He understood full well who He was, but not yet all of what that might mean. And so, with His baptism still dripping off His chin, He strode straight into the wilderness — was "thrown" into the wilderness, the Greek text says — there to be tempted by Satan. The tempter knew well enough who Jesus was and so tried to subvert His mission.

"Command these stones to be made bread. Satisfy Your own shrinking belly and the hunger of Your people. That's what good kings do, after all; they feed the people."

"Cast Yourself down — amaze the masses and prove who You are by demonstrations of self-serving, self-protecting power. That's what the people want, after all — bread and circuses."

"Worship me—God can have the world. Take this shortcut to where You are headed anyway. If You are—since You are—the Son of God, prove it."

"No," Jesus said each time, but slowly, as the temptations were real, the logic credible. But saying no to the tempter and his ways helped Jesus say yes to God and His ways.[34]

All Jesus' tempters, even those of His own disciples then and now, ask Him the same thing, really, in one form or another: "If You are . . . since You are . . . prove it by me—by my nation, my health, my finances. Let me see Your power by what You give me."

One day, a large crowd followed Jesus. Late in the afternoon the tired disciples suggested that Jesus dismiss the people so that the disciples could go into the neighboring villages and buy food. They wanted Jesus to themselves. He was their Lord; they were His servants. Their concern had boundaries, limits. Not everyone was included. But Jesus would have none of it. When Jesus said, "You give them something to eat," He was as much as telling them that the crowds were part of the family, had a place at the table. Even if the disciples saw that part of it, they did not see how all the people could be fed. "One little boy has five loaves and two fish," Andrew said. Just a bag lunch. "But what is that among so many?" The disciples could see only scarcity, what they didn't have, could imagine only what they couldn't do.

Jesus, the gracious Host. He had the people sit down and He blessed the food—and there was plenty. More than enough for everyone. So much that they had to gather the leftovers in baskets.[35] Some scholars read this text and say it was those very loaves and fish that were miraculously multiplied. That may very well be—a once-upon-a-time miracle for the folk who were there. But other scholars have suggested that when people saw what the little boy did and how Jesus blessed him for it, they began sharing their bag lunches too, suddenly neither too afraid nor too selfish to do so.

If in the first interpretation the miracle is unique and unrepeatable, bespeaking Jesus' compassion and power, in the second the miracle is repeatable and fashioned from Jesus' power to change not just loaves but our hearts as well. When we follow His example of faith and give of our best to the Master and each other, we have more than enough to spare. When we let go of our fear, when we see the stranger as neighbor, the outsider as insider—all of that hard work, to be sure—we find that our desire to do as Jesus does blesses others—fills empty stomachs and softens hard hearts. Our own hearts are softened too, as we leave exclusion behind.

Sometime after John was arrested, Jesus marched into Galilee to proclaim the gospel of the kingdom of God: "The time is fulfilled, and the kingdom of God is at hand; repent, and believe in the gospel."[36] Everyone could repent, Jesus said. Everyone *had* to repent. Neither blessing nor warning was exclusive.

Tax collectors heard the message and knew that profit was not wage enough in exchange for a life. Fishermen heard and suddenly knew that life could no longer consist of nets and baits, boats and what they could catch from beneath the surface of the sea. Not after Jesus had hooked them deep in their hearts.

Simon and Andrew were wading in the shallows as they cast their nets. It is a parable, this description of the two. James and John did have a boat, or at least their father, Zebedee, did, and they had helpers too, hired hands. They worked the deeper waters. Were the four fishermen competitors? Rivals? Enemies? We don't know. The text does not tell us. All it says is that Jesus passed by the Sea of Galilee, and He saw the four of them, two by two. He called. They followed and the hardest learning commenced.

In the early morning mist of Galilee's sea there was clarity and, except for the weather and the haul, predictability. Everyone knew the pecking order. Simon and Andrew had their favorite spot, while James and John knew where to dock. They knew the language and the layout, the customs and the customers, the routine and its reasons. Leaving the mist to follow Jesus meant entering a veritable fog, and for three years they did not know what to think or do, what to say or to whom. They had to learn a new way of talking, of thinking, of relating to each other and everyone else.

Jesus kept confusing them: "The one who has it all has nothing;[37] the one who has nothing on account of Me is rich beyond accounting.[38] Those who are not for us are against us;[39] those who are not against us are for us.[40] You have learned to do what Moses said; I am telling you to do more and better."[41]

Jesus invited others to join the group, to be His disciples, and among the rest a Roman collaborator *and* a political revolutionary set on the occupation's overthrow. There was uncertainty and confusion and no pecking order they could discern, as Jesus loved all of them. He seemed to expect each of them to love all the others, just as He did, and so they tried to learn.

"Friends," Jesus said. "I do not call you servants, but friends.[42] You are My friends, and you are each other's friends, and you shall love each other as you never loved before, in the same way I love you."

Jesus and His first disciples, the four fishermen, began traveling together. One day the five of them went to Capernaum. Jesus taught in the synagogue and then a little later went to the home of Simon and Andrew—presumably the poorer pair of Jesus' first disciples—where Jesus healed Simon's mother-in-law, who also seems to have lived there. Jesus "entered the house . . . with James and John," Mark tells us,[43] and we might wonder why he makes a point of it. After all, they have been together for several verses now, and no reader would picture it otherwise. Or does Mark want us to take note? Following Jesus means we travel with people we might never have imagined—competitors and rivals and even enemies are now friends.

Following Jesus means going into homes that, for any number of reasons, we might have avoided before—my home is your home and your home, wherever it might be, is mine.

Following Jesus means we reject rejection, drop old distinctions, and abandon our prejudice.

We will be known by a new company and a borderless geography and a new way of looking at people and things. We have all things in common—friends, resources, homes—because we have Jesus in common.

Nothing more than Him. And by grace nothing less.

But it is hard, this reorientation of relationships and values. Jesus called tax collectors and Zealots, the educated and the unschooled. He dined with the religious authorities and brought with Him others who had trouble with authority (especially religious authority). He was equally serene in the presence of Pharisees and prostitutes and expected His disciples to feel likewise.

The kingdom of God, He said, is like a net holding all sorts of fish.[44] The kingdom of God is like the ark, He could have said, where predators and prey occupy the same cage—but the Flood canceled all bets, changed things, reconfigured all relationships. The kingdom of God overflows Judaism's banks and overturns the customary ways of relating. Who should have been friends turn out to be enemies. Old enemies are new friends.

One day Jesus took with Him Peter, James, and John, and they climbed up a mountainside where Jesus was "transfigured" before them.[45] What that means, exactly, only the four of them know for sure, but one way or the other, something remarkable happened. Jesus' clothes and flesh and presence glowed so that He did not look human anymore, really, at least not the way humans normally look. Suddenly Moses and Elijah were there too, talking with Him about what would happen not many days ahead, when Jesus would climb another mountain, alone this time except for the soldiers and the others bearing crosses. He would be transfigured again—again, He would not look human, at least not in the way people normally look human—His flesh torn and His blood all but bled-out, ruined beyond recognition.

Moses and Jesus and Elijah were talking about all of that when Peter said, "Lord, it is good for us to be here," by which maybe he meant it is better to be *here* than to be *there*, if he had any sense of where *there* was or why they were headed that way. The text says he did not know what he was saying when he said, "Let's build some little shrines, one for you and one for the others, and let's stay."

We like it here. We like how this feels. This is what being a disciple is all about. Forget the world below. This little enclave is sufficient unto itself.

Jesus didn't fuss, not yet, but neither could He stay there, and they would have to follow Him if they wanted to be with Him. So they left and went down the mountain, the glow having dissipated.

When they got to the bottom, they found that in Jesus' absence—and whatever else this story means, it is a parable—the remaining disciples had been unable to help the epileptic son of a distraught father. The man and the disciples were arguing, and Jesus seemed annoyed, as if He too would rather be back up on the mountain than there dealing with that. "I brought my son to Your disciples," the man said, "but they could not do anything for him. If You are able, please heal him."

It is as if the man had seen so much of the incompetence of Jesus' followers that he doubted Jesus too.

"If *I* am able?" Jesus snorted. As if to say to the man, "Do you have any idea to whom you are talking? All things are possible to the one who believes," and though generations of interpretations have misconstrued this text, Jesus was talking about Himself. All things are possible for Jesus, for He is the one, the only one, who *does* believe. The man, to his credit, admitted what all of us need to confess, that all things are not possible because we do not all believe, or do not believe it all: "I believe," he said. "Help my unbelief."

So Jesus worked the miracle, His disciples proving unable to do what Jesus had given them the authority to do: heal.[46]

Jesus then walked on ahead while the disciples had a dispute among themselves. When He asked them what they were arguing about, they got very quiet, embarrassed, for they were arguing as to who was the greatest. Who understood the most of the little they understood, maybe, or who deserved to sit at Jesus' right hand or His left.

Sometime after that, John told Jesus, "Teacher, we saw a man casting out demons in your name, and we forbade him, because he was not following us."[47] The irony could not be more overwhelming: The disciples could not do, prevented others from doing, and still argued as to who among them was the greatest. We hear the echo of Jesus' lament, "O faithless generation, how long am I to put up with you? How long am I to bear with you?"[48]

Only to the end, as it turns out. "Having loved his own who were in the world, he loved them to the end."[49] An amazing grace. A merciful hospitality.

In many places I visit, I see the poem "Footprints in the Sand" by Mary Stevenson Zangare. The climax and comfort come at the end when Jesus says, "The times when you have seen only one set of footprints in the sand, is when I carried you."

Yes, yes. I understand and believe. When we are in the wilderness, when we are down and low, when we are anguished and sorrowful and defeated, Jesus does indeed carry us. That is the consolation of our faith.

But I have been thinking that, unfortunately, consolation is the most many of us want from our faith. We want comfort, assurance, healing, and health. We want God to bless us "real good," to expand our territory, to rapture us away from here when the going gets really rough. We want to be carried, one way or the other, one place to the other, and so we like that image of just one set of footprints in the sand. We like Jesus being our "personal" Savior.

But Jesus comes to the Sea of Galilee, preaching the gospel of God, and He calls—to whomever, He calls—and there are four who answer. Four who follow Jesus, who add their footprints to His on the sand. If there is a picture of what it means to follow Jesus, it is this: footprints in the sand, many sets of footprints—not just one set, not just Him carrying us, but many sets of footprints, seeking Him, finding Him, following Him. The Magi, the man with the withered hand, the fishermen, all of their feet moving toward Jesus, His grace the gravity that pulls them close and keeps them there.

For a while, anyway.

Affirmation: Jesus is not only King of the Jews but Savior of *the world.*

Confession: We want Jesus to be ours alone (self, Church, nation).

Discipleship Task: To see how Jesus loves *the world* and to follow Him by moving from an exclusive to an inclusive faith.

Lent [Middle English *lente* springtime, Lent, from Old English *lencten*; akin to Old High German *lenzin* spring]: the 40 weekdays from Ash Wednesday to Easter observed by the Roman Catholic, Eastern, and some Protestant churches as a period of penitence and fasting

Chapter 4

From Entitlement to Selflessness

Lent

Cure Thy children's warring madness,
Bend our pride to Thy control.
Shame our wanton selfish gladness,
Rich in things and poor in soul.
Grant us wisdom, grant us courage,
Lest we miss Thy kingdom's goal,
Lest we miss Thy kingdom's goal.

— Harry Emerson Fosdick

Their world asked, "How can I get more?" The Desert Fathers
asked, "What can I do without?" Their world asked, "How
can I find myself?" The Desert Fathers asked, "How can I
lose myself?" Their world asked, "How can I win friends and
influence people?" The Desert Fathers asked, "How can I love
God?"

— Richard J. Foster

Mortification is the intentional denial of legitimate pleasures
in the spirit of Christian poverty that one might become more
human. In my tradition Lent has long been considered a time

for mortification, although one would not use such a "medieval" word. We gave up eating, desserts, going to movies, or telling dirty jokes, all of which in the face of world problems seemed rather trivial. Once rendered silly, we dismissed the idea of "giving up" and talked of "taking on." What we failed to understand was that a life incapable of significant sacrifice is also incapable of courageous action.

— URBAN T. HOLMES III

The day of Jesus' circumcision, Simeon could see it all coming—the blood and the tears, the war and the peace, the wounds and the healing—and all of it so clearly he knew he could die happy.

"Master," Simeon prayed as he held the baby Jesus toward Heaven, "now you are dismissing your servant in peace, according to your word."[1] Others had dismissed him as well, and who could blame them? Prophets are without honor in their own precincts, and especially if those precincts belong to the temple.

I picture Simeon as an old man, for some reason, with bits of food in his beard, tattered robes and wild eyes—not scary so much as strange, obsessed. Did he come to the temple every day or just that day? He was waiting for a sign, he said, believed he would see the Lord's Christ before he himself tasted death, and that had to be soon, he figured, old as he was.

I also imagine that most of the faithful who frequented the temple ignored Simeon as best they could — that, or rolled their eyes — discounting both his presence and his prescience, his predictions and his prayers.

Eight days after Jesus' birth, as Luke tells us, Mary and Joseph brought their infant Son to Jerusalem to be circumcised in accordance with the Law. That same day Simeon came to the temple and saw them, the Holy Family — Mary, Joseph, and the prayer-named child. Mary and Joseph's faithfulness to the customs handed down since the time of Abraham brought Jesus to the city and to this moment in the temple. Simeon's trust in the Holy Spirit's words, his hope for Israel and the world, prompted him to greet the Holy Family as they arrived.

He took — *took* — the child from Mary's arms and, one imagines, began to dance and sing a glad, new song to God: "My eyes have seen your salvation, which you have prepared in the presence of all peoples, a light for revelation to the Gentiles and for glory to your people Israel."[2]

Did anyone else notice what the old man was doing, listen to his song, take note of his dance, and wonder what it all might mean? Mary and Joseph must have shivered as Simeon sang and capered about. *They* knew who their Son was but were unaware anyone beyond Bethlehem's shepherds did. They *knew* He was set apart for God's work, but they were not yet certain what that work might entail. But Simeon could see it all: the light and the glory . . . and also the darkness and shame.

His face suddenly lost its smile, his feet their rhythm. Tears, though, remained in his eyes and on his cheeks as he held Jesus close to his chest and warned, "This child is destined for the falling and the rising of many in Israel, and to be a sign that will be opposed." Simeon could already see the wars of words, the resentments and rejections, the end. He knew that this ritual wounding in the temple was but the first Jesus would suffer at the hands of the religious leaders, these drops but the first blood He would spill in obedience to God's command.

"And a sword will pierce your own soul too," Simeon said, very quietly now, to Mary, who must have shivered again. Her baby's life was too new for her to have considered His death. Nor could she yet conceive that her child, flesh of her flesh, was appointed to an ancient and dangerous work. Who could imagine this baby's end? Certainly not His mother.

Simeon might die in peace but the child would not, and I suspect Simeon could see that too. But the child would be for the healing of the world. Jesus' death would give way to life, and so Simeon could die in peace. Any time now.

Lent begins on Ash Wednesday, just over six and one-half weeks before Easter. It is a season apart, a tithe of the year as some have called it, a time to give ourselves, join ourselves more closely to Jesus. For forty days plus Sundays we remember that the one born King of the Jews and Savior of the world will suffer to do God's will in the world, and that those who follow Him must suffer with Him and die with Him, if it comes to that.

"If they hate Me, they will hate you," Jesus warned His followers. "If you follow Me, you can take nothing with you for the journey but a cross. That you have to have with you at all times."[3] We take up the cross daily, but for these forty days we take it up even more, or try to.

At the altar my parishioners kneel, and on each forehead I smudge dark gray ash—what is left of the fronds we used last Palm Sunday, burned for this very purpose. I say to each in turn, "From dust you came, to dust you shall return. Repent and believe the gospel." My ashen touch is a reminder, first, that we and the whole world are dust, that everything we consider permanent will be ash at the last, and, second, that we must live our lives accordingly. Kneeling to receive the ashes at all is a confession that most days we live otherwise.

"Lay not up for yourselves treasure on earth," Jesus said, but we often do.

"If you have two coats in your closet," said Jesus' cousin John, "give one to the poor," but we most often do not.

"Blessed are the poor and woe to you who are rich," Jesus said, but our brokers have convinced us otherwise.

We imagine ourselves needy, sometimes, but Lent demands we tell the truth, that most of us have more than we need, are loathe to share the least of what we have.

There was a rich man[4]—already rich—who suffered a crisis of plenty. His fields produced a record crop, and he had nowhere to store the extra. Perplexed as to what to do—apparently it never occurred to him to share with those whose fields were fallow—he built new barns and thanked, if not God, then the seasons and his lucky stars, that while many were struggling, he had enough to live well and die comfortably. "I wish everyone had as much as I," he might have said and sincerely considered himself blessed, this windfall of grain a special gift to him, a sign of his faithfulness or worth. A reward, even, a token of God's appreciation. In any case this man's theology, if he had one, did not govern his prosperity.

A fool, Jesus called him, and I nod condescending assent. How easy to see this man's silliness and presumption, that one cannot serve God and money, that God's blessings are to be shared. "Do not judge," Jesus said, "but consider your own sin before you see the sin of another."

We are all of us rich fools, truth be told, though sometimes

we pretend we are otherwise: either poor or wise. Lent's impera-
tive, however, is that we confess our own silliness and presumption, identify and repent of the crookedness in us. Lent demands we
acknowledge both that we need straightening and that we cannot
straighten ourselves. We cannot bring down the mountains of pride
and entitlement that ward our hearts, cannot fill the deep moats of
fear and greed that at once protect our *stuff* and separate us from our
needy neighbors.

So we come to the altar to pray. To remember who we really
are and are not, who we are called to be, and whom we are called
to serve. We set ourselves apart during this set-apart time to begin
a season of hard, sacrificial work in hopes that by grace we can
move, or be moved, from pride to humility, from presumption to
repentance, from judgment to confession. Lent calls us to leave our
self-serving and our sense of entitlement behind us and to follow
Jesus by setting our face toward selflessness and sacrifice. "Though
[Jesus] was in the form of God," Paul writes, "He did not cling to
that but opened His hands, opened His heart, poured Himself out,
emptied Himself for the sake of God's will and God's love for the
world."[5] We try to do likewise, a little. We pray that we might be
so filled with the goodness of God that we want for nothing else,
especially the doomed treasures of the world. We make a small hole
in our lives, open a crack in our days, give up something for the sake
of Him who gave up everything in order that a bit of light might
seep in, that holiness be born in us.

What can we give to the God who has all things? Only what we
take from ourselves.

Ours is a small sacrifice, usually—and trivial, if you look at
it one way (how does giving up Cokes or chocolate or movies help
the world?)—and yet it is a patterned obedience, a willful sacrifice.
When we take something away from our lives and give it to God,
we are creating a space. Taking away one more barrier between

Him and ourselves. We are relying, in one more way, on God's sufficiency.

Thursday night in the Steagald house was always vocabulary night. For years, one or the other of the kids had a vocabulary test on Friday morning, and early on we got into a pattern of preparation. Jo, my wife, would take blank index cards, and on one side of each she would put the word in big, block letters, while on the other side she would write the definition of the word. She would then begin the work, showing first the word or the definition, then having the children call back to her the other.

Jesus adopted a similar strategy with His disciples in view of the test that was coming. In Caesarea Philippi, a town far north of Jerusalem but no city of refuge, Jesus began coaching, teaching, schooling His friends on what awaited them all, but most especially awaited Him. Time was running out, and soon enough they would be in the Holy City where unholy currents would swirl all around them, take them under. Soon enough they would hear all manner of things said about Jesus, lies and accusations and slander, and soon enough they would themselves be called upon to give testimony as to who He was and what He was doing.

Jesus tried to ready the disciples. He gave them definitions, called out words, tried to teach them what they needed to know. But they were for the moment clueless, as if Jesus was speaking a foreign language. And of course He was.

In Caesarea there were lots of shrines to various gods. The busy city sat on a bustling crossroads, trade routes from here to there intersecting. Many different kinds of people from many different kinds of places with many different ways of worshiping many different kinds of gods made Caesarea a different kind of place, and the local chamber of commerce was intent on making everybody feel right at home. No surprise then to find numerous churches, numerous temples and shrines, and plenty of pluralism and tolerance attending.

In the midst of all this syncretism, Jesus asked the disciples His second most famous question: "Who do men say that the Son of man is?" And while the disciples were stammering about, trying to impress the Teacher, guessing as to what everyone else's index card had on the back—John the Baptist, said some, Elijah, said others, or another prophet—Jesus asked His first most famous question: "But who do you say I am?"

"You are the Christ," Peter said, "the Son of the living God."

"Correct!" Jesus said. "One hundred percent. Blessed are you, Simon Johnson![6] For flesh and blood has not revealed this to you, but my Father who is in heaven."[7] Simon got a gold star and a smiley face. And now that he knew the words, Jesus as much as said, "Let's turn the card over and learn the definition."

Three times in two chapters Jesus taught the disciples a definition of "Christ," or its synonym, "Son of Man." "The Son of man must suffer many things, and be rejected by the elders and the chief priests and the scribes, and be killed, and after three days rise again. And he said this plainly."[8] But Simon did not like this lesson, didn't like it for Jesus or for himself. Peter jerked Jesus aside, rebuked the Teacher. "Quit talking like that," Peter insisted. "It is not going to happen. You are not going to Jerusalem, and you are not going to die, and neither are we."

Although Jesus was willing to suffer at the hands of the elders and the priests and others, He was unwilling to suffer such foolishness as this. So He pushed right back, changed Peter's grade to F: "Get *behind* me, Satan, for you are thinking in earthly terms, not heavenly." Peter could not get the definition on the back of the

Son-of-Man card, did not understand what "Christ" meant beyond the conventional wisdom he had been taught.

How like Peter we are. We too would love for Jesus' identity to offer protection and benefit to His disciples—then and now—and it does, but not as His disciples are sometimes inclined to imagine. We are drawn to the blessings of following Jesus, not the cost. We covet the security, not the risk. We are tempted to imagine that our faithfulness and devotion provide, cause and effect, tangible rewards—not only Heaven in the end but other things, worldly goods, quantifiable and visible. "Nothing too good for the servants of the Lord," we might say to ourselves, which is also to say, "Nothing too bad for the servants of the Lord." We do not much want to believe that following Jesus can mean suffering and sacrifice, that what is most visible to disciples may be the cross up ahead on the hilltop, and most tangible the nails waiting for our hands.

For the Ash Wednesday service one year, I asked Birk to make a cross. He told me he had some old dogwood limbs that would be perfect. I asked him to cut six holes in the cross, once he had it formed, one for each of the purple candles I planned to light each Sunday as we made our way through Lent. As good a woodworker as Birk was, he barely got the cross made and could not drill the holes at all. It was as if the cross refused the light. The wood was too hard, he said, too old. He broke several drill bits and his pride in the process.

I lugged the cross in from the sacristy, scarred with Birk's futility and heavy, leaned it against the Table for everyone to see. I told them what Birk said.

Later, during my meditation and right before the imposition of ashes, I took from the pulpit a gift given me by a priest, a small black cross inlaid with twenty or thirty pieces of a shattered mirror, all of them close together so that when anyone would look at the cross closely they would see themselves, but broken.

Indeed we are broken, all of us. The cross in my hand, like the cross in our sanctuary, shows as much if we really look, and even if we don't. There is a disconnect between head and heart, between heart and life. Our speech is crooked, and mine especially so. My guilt is double because I know better, or should, at least a little. Lent allows me, compels me, to confess how my theological precision grows dull and rusty, how the storehouse of my heavenly treasure is home to rats, how my convictions leak and muddy my prayers.

The preacher in the tailored suit and crocodile shoes glides across my television screen, his smile incandescent and his tone reassuring. I reject his message outright. I renounce any theology that dares to suggest my best life is now. I decry any preaching or teaching that affirms I can have it all—treasure on earth and treasure in Heaven—or, even more preposterously, that God *wants* me to have it all. "You cannot serve God and wealth,"[9] Jesus said, but some preach that both serve us.

I protest, bark at the smiling preacher on the TV, who does not blink at my rebuke. "For our sakes, Jesus became poor,"[10] I spit. Why? So that for His sake we could be rich? Well, yes, that is what Paul said, but rich so that we can be generous, give to others, fill another's barns or give away our coats and cloaks. Many of the least of these, Jesus' brothers and sisters, are poor and naked and homeless. Will I dress in finery as they suffer?

What I am watching on TV looks less like worship than it does an Amway convention. I am boiling.

The Westminster Shorter Catechism's first question is this: "What is the chief end of man?" And the answer is, "Man's chief end is to glorify God, and to enjoy Him forever." I decry any suggestion that there is a lesser end—not our enjoying God but that God's chief end is to enable us to enjoy the goods of the world.

My indignation is fierce . . . when suddenly I remember that on my forehead is a smudge of ash. Almost against my will I recall how last year I lobbied for a big raise. "I need to make more money than I am making," I said to the chairman of the personnel committee, meaning really that I *want* to make more than I am making, that I think I deserve it. Before the meeting I had compared my salary and benefits, not to the many below me, but to the relatively few above me, and had written them down for reference. Pride and entitlement reminded the committee how hard I work, how much education I have.

Next, I remembered how many times I have ladled a thick gravy of derision on those who have written and read and prayed the prayer of Jabez—better to write and read and pray the *Lord's* Prayer instead, I sniff—but I had to confess that I myself have asked God to enlarge my sales at Borders.

I regularly slam those who are suffering from a particularly American form of entitlement but acknowledge that I myself feel entitled to so many things. I pray, after all. I serve Christ in the Church. I ought to get some perk, some currency or benefit from that relationship, shouldn't I?

I reject that TV-preaching thinking, boast a different theology, but I confess that my theology does not always govern my prayers, that "success" leaks into my petitions. I confess all this to my friend Jonathan, who says serenely, "No one is consistent." I wish the problem were that benign. I am full of holes and contradictions. I am ash and dust. I am mountains and valleys.

Not everyone wants a suffering King. Not everyone desires God's peculiar form of prosperity—the one who is poor is rich, the one who is a failure is a success, the one who is rejected is accepted, the one who would be first of all must be last of all and servant of all.[11]

Mountains do not want to be brought low, and those who easily walk crooked roads are not eager for the bulldozers to appear. No surprise then that opposition and rejection, quarrels and contention, attend Jesus' mission almost from the start.

Among the most unsettling of His quarrels comes from His own disciples. Over and over again they either do not understand or they understand well enough but are reluctant, even resistant, to follow where He leads. They hear His words but do not allow them to sink deeper than that. Though time and time again Jesus tried to tell them that His suffering was inevitable, even necessary—and that their own sacrifices were part of the job description of a disciple—they did not want to believe or follow in that way. They rather imagined that being intimates of the Messiah entitled them to certain perks, payoffs, benefits, and protections.

One day James and John asked Him, "Make us to sit, one on Your right and one on Your left, when You come into Your kingdom. If You are a king, since You are a king, grant our petition." Or maybe it was their mother who made the request,[12] but either way neither James nor John nor anyone else knew that Jesus' coronation would be His crucifixion; to be at His right or left meant being crucified with Him. "If anyone would find his life he must lose his life."[13] Well, where is the fun in that?

Sometime after His baptism and time of testing in the wilderness, Jesus came back to Nazareth, where He had been raised. He had been preaching for a while already, had already received some acclaim and recognition, and so it was no surprise when He went to His hometown synagogue on the Sabbath, He was given the scroll to read. He found and read a passage in Isaiah:

> The Spirit of the Lord is upon me,
> because he has anointed me to preach good news to the poor.
> He has sent me to proclaim release to the captives
> and recovering of sight to the blind,
> to set at liberty those who are oppressed,
> to proclaim the acceptable year of the Lord.[14]

Everyone in the synagogue liked this passage, but when Jesus began preaching, things got ugly. His listeners were thinking, *Do here what you did in Capernaum. After all, you are home now and that is where charity begins. Bless your kinfolk first; take care of those nearest to you.*

Jesus, though, reminded His friends and kin that God had healed a *Syrian* king's leprosy and had not healed the many Israelites who were lepers. There is no border on God's grace, He as much as said. He recalled how during a great famine God had sent the prophet Elijah to feed a Gentile widow living in Sidon of Zarepheth, all the while Israelite widows went hungry. There is no special privilege or entitlement for one group over another—that seemed the gist of His message for the day. No special protection for those who are called.

At the beginning of the sermon, all in the synagogue looked at Jesus favorably, considered His words gracious. By the end they were enraged, ready to kill Him for daring to preach such a message. They rushed Him, forced Him to the prow of the cliff on which Nazareth was built, were ready to throw Him off the cliff.

But Jesus "passed through the midst of them" and went on His way. Moses' parting the Red Sea was no more miraculous, a professor of mine used to say. Soon, though, the sea of Jesus' enemies would close round Him again, and He would not escape.

Many of Jesus' sermons and stories, many of His miracles and the places He performed them, laid a parabolic ax to the root of long-assumed certainties. Jesus said that the religious leaders were like wicked tenants, and the hookers and tax collectors first in line at the kingdom's door. Jesus said that though some had said "yes" to God's call and command, they had failed to do as they promised, while others had said "no," yet were being obedient in spite of themselves.

One can only imagine that from Jesus' perspective there was hope that a new shoot of faithfulness, trellised by the Spirit more than the Law, by mercy more than justice, would grow up among God's people. We do not have to guess, however, how the Pharisees and the Sadducees regarded Jesus' teaching. Or how they planned to deal with it.

"[They] took counsel . . . how they might destroy him," Mark tells us.[15] And if both Jesus and the religious leaders could see it coming—as Simeon had, long years before—Jesus' followers for the most part could not begin to imagine what was about to transpire.

Affirmation: Jesus is a "sign to be opposed," as His ministry proves dangerous.

Confession: We want Jesus to ensure our success, wealth, and health.

Discipleship Task: To hear the call to self-denial and to follow Jesus by moving from entitlement to selflessness.

Advent

Christmas

Epiphany

Lent

Holy Week : the week before Easter during which the last days of Christ's life are commemorated

Easter

Pentecost

Trinity

Ordinary Time

Christ the King

Chapter 5

From Fear to Surrender

Holy Week

How can we serve a Lord, the symbol of whose failure is above
our altars, on top of our churches, on our stationery, and around
our necks, and claim to be a stranger to failure?

—URBAN T. HOLMES III

The cross is such a hard, hard piece of the gospel that most of us
cannot stay converted to it for long.

—BARBARA BROWN TAYLOR

Holy Week is like the rest of Lent, only more intense. Every day there is a story of conflict. Every day there is a drama of redemption. The fear that has accompanied the disciples along the way of late[1] is only heightened. Everyone is afraid—the authorities, the disciples, and perhaps even Jesus.

He did not want to happen what He knew was going to happen, but He "set his face to go to Jerusalem,"[2] Luke writes, knowing full well all that awaited Him there. Yet Jesus moved past His fear to surrender—"not my will, but thine, be done"[3]—and He seemed to expect that His disciples would too.

He had warned them: "Let these words sink into your ears." Into your hearts as well, He might have said. "The Son of man is to be delivered into the hands of men."[4] But the warning did not suffice. The disciples' fear remained. They did not ask Jesus what He meant. They did not want to know.

Palm/Passion Sunday: The Triumphal Entry

Tell the daughter of Zion,
Look, your king is coming to you,
     humble, and mounted on a donkey,
          and on a colt, the foal of a donkey.[5]

Matthew reads Zechariah's prophecy literally, not poetically. He tells us that the disciples brought the donkey and the colt to Jesus and put their cloaks on them, and that Jesus rode on both of them as He began His descent into Jerusalem. It is an almost comedic scene, and tragic too, as Jesus tries to ride both animals at once. Different heights, different gaits, Jesus bounces along, tries hard to maintain His balance.

We do too as we try to stay astride both Palm Sunday truths: Jesus is coming at last, but He is coming to die. Do we celebrate? Do we cry? Are we happy? Are we afraid?

Yes.

Father Charles comes to the community Palm Sunday service in a flowing red cape that billows out behind him in the breeze. He is a very large man, and the cape is larger as he seems to fly or float through the crowd solemnly gathered in the middle of Main Street to hear and read the Palm Sunday Scriptures.

Red is the color of festival, of fire and celebration—Jesus is come to Jerusalem! Behold your King! The other ministers and I appear underdressed, out of sync with Father Charles and this news. Soon, though, when the mood and the lessons have suddenly shifted from red to purple and black (as we read accounts of the trial, the suffering, the death of Jesus), Father Charles will be the one overdressed, out of sync, unless the red flowing down his back and pooling at his feet represents blood.

In former generations, Palm Sunday was a commemoration unto itself. Preachers read of Jesus' entry alone: how He sent the disciples for the donkey, how the owner released it for Jesus' purposes, how the disciples placed Jesus on it and put down palm branches and robes for the donkey to walk on. Perhaps they read of Jesus' weeping over Jerusalem too, but the assumption was that worshipers would be back for more services that week, for Maundy Thursday and Good Friday, especially. The dark stories could wait until their hour had come.

But people got busy. Many of the faithful came back only on Easter—the very next Sunday—and so to ensure that they did not go from glory to glory, triumph to triumph, parade to Resurrection, the decision was made to read also the dark texts on Palm Sunday.

Father Charles in his red, me in my purple, Herb and Jerry in their black suits. Festivity and mourning, celebration and lamentation, all of it together this day. Jesus is King; there is an assassination plot underway. It is hard to ride the mismatched realities brought to us this day. We are unbalanced, unsettled, unsure as to what it all might mean.

We do not know, not all of it anyway, and like Jesus' disciples we are often afraid to ask beyond the obvious, what goes on here.

Jesus began to descend the Mount of Olives and the disciples "began to rejoice and praise God with a loud voice for all the mighty works that they had seen."[6] They sang, they danced, they whooped it up big. It may have been a small parade, but it was festive enough that some of the Pharisees who saw it fussed at Jesus, told Him to get control of His disciples. "Tell them to shut up!" they as much as said. "This display is unseemly." Jesus replied, "If these were silent, even the stones would cry out." And so they will, so they will.

Soon, very soon, there will be an earthquake,[7] shifting ground. Even as other, louder voices drowned out the praise, a great silence will engulf the earth and the sun will be blown out like a candle. The world will tilt and everyone, disciples and enemies alike, will lose their footing, lose their sight, be scared almost to death. Or to life.

As Jesus drew near Jerusalem, He cried over it. "Would that even today you knew the things that make for peace!" Jesus wept because only one thing could make for peace, and it meant the ruin of Him. Jesus wept because His enemies were only too eager to do that ruinous work, imagining that His solitary suffering would somehow save the nation. He wept because, in fact, His death would do just that, but not in ways His enemies understood.

What the people seem to have wanted was a king like David, a warrior who would bring peace through war, freedom through victory, the death of Israel's occupiers and enemies. What Jesus offered was peace through surrender, freedom through defeat, and life for all by His willingness to die.

Jesus on a donkey. He is on a protest march though even the disciples did not realize it at first. Jesus is protesting against the grandiose and militaristic expectations of those who learned to translate *Messiah* in terms of stallions and swords and wars. The parade is a funeral procession too, though Jesus alone seems to understand this.

Jesus did not explain what He was doing; He just did it. He did not justify His actions or interpret them; He remained silent, kept His own counsel, though the world was abuzz around Him. Some were in a frenzy, others in a panic. Some said He was the Son of David, the King of the Jews. Others said He was an imposter, a pretender, an insurrectionist. For some He was Immanuel, God with us: the Christ, the Holy One, the Son of the Living God. For others, He was Beelzebub, the Devil, an iconoclast and threat. Some hailed Him, others rebuked Him; some wanted to crown Him, others wanted to kill Him.

But Jesus said not a word.

He let the crowds, His friends, His enemies, make of Him what they would—king, a criminal, a victim, or even a sacrifice. He still does.

MONDAY: THE CONFRONTATION IN THE TEMPLE

John tells the story of Jesus' confrontation in the temple early in his gospel,[8] right after the wedding in Cana. John is sounding a tone, playing an overture whose themes will be spelled out later: that following Jesus means both wine-drinking good times and blood-chilling confrontations. There is no joy like the joy of being with Jesus and no danger so great as being His disciple. Following Him is peace; following Him is war.

One can only imagine how the disciples must have felt in either case.

Elated, perhaps, about their Teacher being the life of the party, able to make a fine Pinot out of plain old well water. They tipped their glasses, toasted the groom, and Jesus, impromptu vintner, joined in on a chorus of "Let the Good Times Roll."

Then terrified when the tables in the temple rolled, when Jesus Himself rolled them and then made a whip of cords and started chasing the money changers out of the place. I can see the disciples huddled in the corner, out of harm's way, their eyes wide and their hearts thumping wildly as animals and bankers, Jesus and priests scurried about. "Zeal for thy house will consume me,"[9] they said later, thinking of Jesus, but just as sure that Jesus' zeal for God's house would consume them too.

"Take these *things* away," Jesus shouted. "You shall not make my Father's house a house of trade."[10] The religious leaders charged Him, demanded explanation and credential. His explanation was cryptic: "Destroy this temple, and in three days I will raise it up."[11] No one knew then that He meant the temple of His body.

The other gospels tell this story later, after the Triumphal Entry,[12] not as preamble but as climax. Jesus arrived in Jerusalem to break up the furniture, the trappings of the religious system as it had come to be. "My house shall be called a house of prayer," Jesus scolded, "but you have made it a 'den of thieves.'"[13] Not just God's house now but His house, Jesus' house. Not just trade, either, but thievery.

From our safe distance it is easy to smile, even laugh, at how Jesus went after the religious professionals in the temple. It can make for smug and fiery preaching for those who want to tear into the Church as it often is—materialistic and self-serving, institutional and legalistic—as opposed to how we think it should be. More difficult, and more important, is to see that Jesus comes after me in the temple of my own heart—which ought to be a place of prayer, of absolute love for and attention to God—to find that I have let thieves set up shop and do their daily work. My mind and my soul as well are full of passions and prejudice, envy and pride, lust and despairing. With my complicity I have allowed those to rob me of true intimacy with God. The one who needs cleansing is me, for I take the clean currency of the gospel and exchange it for pennies on the dollar.

The scouring Jesus offers terrifies and thrills. I would my soul to be clean, my prayers just the same. But I fear I am not prepared to lose what must be driven from my heart, my dear and familiar idols. I am caught, sure that one way or the other—with Jesus at the hands of the religious leaders who brook no dissent, or at the hands of Jesus Himself who suffers no fools—I am about to die.

Tuesday: The Time Has Come

It was Passover, one of the major festivals, one that all Jews no matter their nationality or language were expected to attend, and the kind of party non-Jews wanted as well. No surprise, then, that there were Greeks at the festival, either faithful Jews living in another land or Gentiles on hand for the camaraderie or commerce. Some of these Greeks, whoever they were and for whatever reason—messianic expectation or mere curiosity—came to one of Jesus' disciples, Philip, himself apparently a Greek speaker, and asked him to arrange an audience for them with Jesus.

Philip told Andrew, and together they went and told Jesus, who seems to have heard in His disciples' words something more significant than their report of a routine conversation with tourists, something much deeper and darker.

"The hour has come for the Son of Man to be glorified," Jesus said. "Very truly, I tell you, unless a grain of wheat falls into the earth and dies, it remains just a single grain; but if it dies, it bears much fruit. Those who love their life lose it, and those who hate their life in this world will keep it for eternal life. Whoever serves me must follow me, and where I am, there will my servant be also."[14]

It was a terrifying word, not least for its suddenness. Only two days before, outside the city on the Mount of Olives, things seemed to have been going well. Now, death hung in the air like an eagle ready to dive, talons bared. Jesus seemed ready to bare His neck, give Himself over to this fate. "Now my soul is troubled. And what should I say—'Father, save me from this hour'? No, it is for this reason that I have come to this hour."[15]

But it was not for this hour that the disciples had come, though surely their souls were troubled as well. Would they have to give themselves up too? Thomas seemed to think so, even before they came to Jerusalem.

When Lazarus fell ill, his sisters summoned Jesus to Lazarus' sickbed in Bethany.[16] But before Jesus got there, Lazarus was dead and buried, and a crowd from Jerusalem, including some of the religious leaders, was present for the funeral. Still a ways off, Jesus told the disciples that their friend Lazarus was dead and that He was going to Bethany to "wake him out of sleep"—to raise him. Thomas, not doubting Jesus could do such a thing, still imagined the worst, that the religious leaders would not stand idly by if Jesus proved to be such a Healer as this. The life of Lazarus would prove the death of Jesus, and Thomas could see it coming. "Let us also go," he said, mustering the other disciples, "that we may die with him,"[17] and perhaps he thought they would die right then, right there in Bethany. His timing was off, we know, but his prescience proved true enough.

Now other disciples can see and know what Thomas saw and knew.

Tuesday in Holy Week is the Lenten form of Epiphany. As the Gentiles came to Jesus and proclaimed His identity by virtue of His birth, the Greeks who came signaled the fulfillment of that identity—His destiny, by virtue of His death. Jesus would be raised up, crucified, and thereby draw all people to Himself.[18] The Greeks' arrival signaled Jesus' coming death. Jesus' word foreshadowed it. The disciples' dread was like confirmation. They could no longer deny what was coming.

WEDNESDAY: THE ANOINTING AT BETHANY

During His time of wilderness trial, Jesus refused the crown Satan offered Him.[19] He also refused the populist enthronements offered Him after He fed the multitudes[20] and as He entered the Holy City of Jerusalem.[21] However, He accepted the scandalous coronation, which was like a prophet's anointing,[22] offered Him by Mary, the sister of His friend Lazarus, when she poured a bottle of expensive oil not on Jesus' head but on His feet.[23]

Her behavior was shocking—no proper woman let her hair down in public—and also surprising. She may have worked years to acquire this oil for the time of her own death, her own embalming. The disciples did not know what to say, how to react. There was only silence as the fragrance of the oils filled the house.

Then Judas Iscariot grew indignant, sputtered his angry words to no one in particular. "This ointment should have been sold!"[24]

The words sounded hollow as he said them. Judas was just a thief, cared only to pilfer the purse if the oil was sold and the proceeds deposited.

Or was it more than that? Different? Maybe he was embarrassed by Mary's devotion, embarrassed for her siblings, their hosts, and for Jesus too? How *inappropriate* when Jesus had so clearly said to the young man, "Sell what you have and give the money to the poor."[25] Perhaps Judas was afraid a reprimand was coming and wanted to appear as if *he* at least understood. Or maybe he wanted to be sure that what Jesus demanded of the young man and of him was required for everyone. If not, he might have made a huge mistake in following when Jesus called.

One way or another, Judas said out loud only what all of the rest of them were thinking.[26]

"Leave her alone," Jesus said. A different reprimand. "What Mary has done for me is a beautiful thing. The poor you always have with you, but you do not always have me."[27] The King will not live long, but the memory of what she has done will.

After the anointing Judas went to the authorities and made a deal to deliver Jesus into their hands.[28] Why did he do that? Why then?

Luke and John, each in his own way, said it was the Devil that made him do it: that Satan put it into Judas's heart to conspire with the authorities to destroy Jesus.[29] Judas either asked for money or money was offered him, and he may have been just that cold, so cash crazy as to sell his friend for a measly thirty pieces of silver.

Or was it something else? As Mary anointed Jesus' feet, He spoke of His death, of His embalming. Jesus had spoken of His death other times, but maybe Judas heard it in a way he never had before, could see the sadness, the resignation in Jesus' face. If he were not merely a thief, not merely a betrayer, but a disciple still, he did not want Jesus to die. He might have imagined that if he could deliver Jesus into the hands of the authorities—into protective custody—then with Passover coming there would be time for everyone to cool down.

Somehow Judas knew the religious leaders and was able to get an appointment on short notice. He knew Jesus too, of course, His habits and movements. Perhaps Judas thought that if Jesus and the leaders could talk, they could get through all this without anyone getting hurt, could reach compromise if not agreement. They all wanted the same things, after all—peace, freedom, God's will to be done on earth as it is in Heaven.

So he struck the deal and the next night, after supper, met the soldiers—armed in case the Romans accosted them—and went to the Garden of Gethsemane to retrieve Jesus, to rescue Him from the growing crisis. Judas was afraid for Jesus, afraid for Israel, afraid for them all. He had to make something happen or everything would be lost.

Whatever he dreamed might happen, though, it was a nightmare soon enough, and the next night, when he realized the custody he had arranged would in no way protect Jesus, that instead the authorities condemned Jesus, Judas gave the money back and tried to undo the deal.[30] It may be that he hanged himself, if that is what he did,[31] because he was also afraid that neither Jesus nor the others would understand what he had hoped, what he had tried to do.

Maybe. Maybe not.

MAUNDY THURSDAY: THE FOOT WASHING, GETHSEMANE, AND THE TRIALS

The Foot Washing

The Last Supper made Jesus' friends face their fears—their fear of intimacy and their fear of separation. Who among them could have said which they feared more?

We fear both things too, I believe—in our relationship with God and in our relationships with each other.

On Thursday evening Jesus changed the command He gave His disciples earlier. Back when the lawyer stood to test Him, to ask Him the greatest commandment, Jesus replied, "You shall love the Lord your God with all your heart, and with all your soul, and with all your mind. This is the great and first commandment. And a second is like it, You shall love your neighbor as yourself."[32] The first command was clear and absolute, unalterable and unchanging. But there was a loophole in the second—wiggle room if we do not love ourselves. So at dinner Jesus tightened the loop, closed the hole: "A new command I give you, that you love one another as I have loved you."[33]

The disciples and Jesus had gathered together one last time, and perhaps they knew it was, in fact, the last time.[34] If it was a Seder meal, as many believe it was—the Passover meal Jews annually observe in memory of God's delivery of the Jews from bondage—it was unlike any they had ever attended. The elements were the same: the lamb and the cups of wine, the bread and *charosis*,[35] the bitter herbs and the story of Moses, the plagues and the lamb, God's mighty hand and outstretched arm. Such was the focus of every Seder meal.

Jesus was host, led them through the ritual meal, but as He did He redefined the Passover story in terms of Himself. "The bread is not just motzo, unleavened to recall the haste of the liberated slaves—it is My body, given for you, a slow sacrifice for your freedom. This wine is not just a sign of God's provision and life given from the earth—it is My blood, poured out for you and for many, a sign of provision and death given from My heart."[36]

And then He washed their feet. Knelt before them who had knelt before Him. He filled a bowl with water, made holy by His touch, and took their feet into His hands and bathed them as if in baptism, as if they were His children. Andrew, Matthew, John, Judas, and the rest, one by one He washed the feet of them all.

It was as scandalous a devotion as Mary's anointing of Him had been, their Teacher and Lord bowing before them as if He were something else, their servant maybe. At first Peter, at least, refused—not because his feet were dirty, but because Jesus was their Lord, their Teacher, the Holy One of God. This amazing intimacy mortified Peter. "You will never wash my feet," he growled, as if to say, "It is I who should wash Your feet, and yet You wash mine?"

"Yes," Jesus says, "I wash your feet." He was telling Peter, much as He had told John the Baptist at the Jordan, "My washing your feet, your having your feet washed, this is righteousness."

Peter's protests and misunderstanding were soon washed away by grace.

The word *Maundy* comes from the Latin word *maundus*, from which we derive the English word *mandate*. Maundy Thursday is Command Thursday, the day of Jesus' mandate that we obey His loophole-closing command and follow His example. "Do you know what I have done for you?" He asked the disciples when He had once again taken His seat. "You call me Teacher and Lord and you are right. That is who I am. If I then have done this for you, you ought also to do this for one another. I have given you an example, that you should also do as I have done for you,"[37] Jesus said, but sadly foot washing is an intimacy most of His disciples never experience, a grace they do not enjoy.

Every Maundy Thursday I schedule a foot washing, but many even of the most faithful church members I serve cannot bring their feet to this service, their lack of ease an echo of Peter's. We fear the intimacy, I think—touching and being touched in a way most of us have not experienced since we bathed our babies or were bathed ourselves. We also fear the separation, what comes after the service, knowing that day by day we are most of us so distant from one another, so alone in our heart of hearts, that we cannot except momentarily love each other as Jesus commands. Almost better not to feel it at all than to feel it and feel it gone.

In those years when I am facing a move to a new church, the service is more painful still, becomes a terrible first good-bye, casts in sharp relief the coming grief.

We gather together around water and the Word, twenty-five chairs in a circle and a hand-turned bowl between us with a post, a small pedestal, in its center. Warm water forms, as it were, a circle in the bowl. I kneel before my people one by one, members of the church and others, some of them friends. I take a bare or sometimes stockinged foot into my hand, and I place it on the pedestal, with cupped hands ladle water onto it. I look straight into the eyes of the ones before whom I kneel, whether they are able to look at me or not. And often they are not. This sharing, this tenderness, can cut deeply, the impending separation deeper still.

I speak of God's love, of Jesus' call, of the grace that is ours as spiritual friends.

Tears sometimes come, gasps, for love of God and one another, for fear of losing that love, losing this moment now that we have come to it. For fear of opening our shut-up hearts and lives to others, even strangers, for fear of the loneliness if we do not—we are doubly afraid, and which of us knows what we fear more?

Gethsemane

After the Meal and the foot washing, Jesus and the disciples made their way to Gethsemane, a garden, a place of refuge and prayer. John, for his own reasons, does not show us Jesus' agony, His terrible tortured prayer that the cup might pass from Him. But the other evangelists do.[38]

Jesus leaves His drowsy disciples, goes off by Himself about a stone's throw, and prays to His Father in Heaven, begs God for the sake of His hallowed name to let His kingdom come and His will be done, yes, of course, but please, God, not in this way. Jesus prays that God will deliver Him from this evil, that the bread God gives Him the next day will not be the bread of suffering but a different bread, the bread of Heaven. "Thine is the power," Jesus knew to pray.

It is almost too much to watch, Jesus on the ground, His clothes damp with dew and His face wet with tears. Maybe that is why John does not show us this scene, wanting us to take comfort in Jesus' serenity and certainty. The other gospel writers, though, seem to want us to know that our own agonized prayers are not without precedent: that Jesus prayed as we have, in fear and finally surrender. "Not my will, but thy will be done."

We hear Jesus' prayer but not God's answer. Unlike other times when Jesus prayed, we see no dove, hear no voice—and neither, apparently, did Jesus—but surely God was well pleased with His Son, who would die as faithfully as He had lived. Somehow, this time, it was the silence itself that gave Jesus strength to surrender.

Sometimes on account of a word, sometimes on account of the silence—we too find strength to surrender to God's will. And in surrender comes victory.

The Trials

When Pilate heard the crowds shout that Jesus had "made himself the Son of God," John tells us that "he was the more afraid,"[39] meaning of course that the powerful Roman official had been afraid from the start.

Herod was afraid too, although he may have tried to cover it with the pancake makeup of political pretense, threats, and farce. His demands were a cracked bell: "Show me a miracle, prove You are the Messiah."[40] Herod had been afraid upon first hearing of Jesus, thinking that John, whom he had beheaded, had returned from the dead.[41]

Herod was a bully, no more, no less. A surprising enemy to Jesus, a fellow Jew. If Herod did not want Jesus dead, he at least wanted Jesus out of his sight. Pilate was more judicious, a manager, attempting damage control to protect his own position. For fear of the supposed insurrectionist, Pilate proved a surprising advocate; he tried to have Jesus released. Then, when that didn't work, for fear of the crowds, he consented to Jesus' death.

The authorities were afraid—of the Romans, the crowds, and of Jesus too, I think, either for fear that He was a blasphemer[42] or that He was not. For fear they would lose their living and way of life, for fear the temple might be destroyed. Better to kill one man, they said, than to have everyone die for Him.[43] And the disciples had fled, for fear of what would happen to Jesus and of what might happen to them.

They were all of them gone, His disciples, except for the one who trailed behind to see what might become of Jesus and Simon Peter with Him.[44] Peter was afraid to admit he knew Jesus. Jesus alone seemed fearless, resigned, surrendered, and serene.

Good Friday: The Flogging, the Way of Sorrows, and the Crucifixion

The Flogging

Why did Pilate have Jesus scourged, parade Him around the Praetorium in purple robes and a crown of thorns?

To humiliate Him? To appease the crowd's blood fever?

Many of the condemned prisoners did not survive the beating.

Hardened soldiers used leather flagellums studded with scrap metal, bone fragments, and stones to peel flesh off the unfortunate's back. Those who survived, if they had strength and sense and senses left to feel anything at all, were surely sorry to have done so.

The soldiers, with barely any more of Jesus' flesh to ruin, savaged His dignity. They dressed Him for display, propped Him up, a ragged caricature, this "king."

Perhaps it occurred to Pilate that the sight of Jesus—"*Ecce homo*," he said, "Just *look* at the man"[45]—ravaged as He was by the hated occupiers, might finally elicit some sympathy on the part of the crowds. He had tried to release Jesus, had tried to release Him again, and nothing had worked. He found no crime in Jesus, he said, nothing deserving death. Could Jesus' near-death satisfy the mob, forge some identification between the crowd and Jesus on account of their common enemy, the Romans? Seeing Him this way might draw some sympathy even from the professionally sympathetic religious leaders.

Nothing worked. Pilate knew that Jesus was right—knew the fearful truth—that he, Pilate, the powerful Roman governor, had no power at all.[46]

The Way of Sorrows

John tells us that Jesus carried His own cross to the place called The Skull, carried that heavy weight on which He would be nailed and splayed for however long it took Him to die.

It is hard to imagine that He had back or blood or strength enough left after the flogging to carry so much as His own weight down the Way of Sorrows, much less a gibbet or even the transom. But John may be speaking theologically as much as historically, saying that Jesus was strong enough to shoulder the sins of the world and His own burdens besides. For his part, Luke says Jesus had help—that a soldier compelled Simon of Cyrene to complete Jesus' journey to Golgotha.

At spear point, or threat of it, Simon of Cyrene took Jesus' cross on his shoulder as his own. Simon may have been an unwilling disciple, but that is what disciples do: They find themselves compelled, one way or the other, to carry Jesus' cross to wherever Jesus will give His life. They do so every time they carry their own cross to where Jesus bids them come and die.

The Crucifixion

"Without the shedding of blood there is no forgiveness of sins," the author of Hebrews writes,[47] which is to say that with the shedding of blood there is forgiveness of sins. At least in the case of the Crucifixion that is the way it happened. Jesus bled. Jesus forgave.

Jesus was hung between Heaven and earth, so much food for the birds. A euphemism for one crucified was "crow bait," and a person might remain on the cross, suspended and naked, for days if the individual was strong enough, struggling to the last for breath enough to imprecate the soldiers and the passersby, to pray for death. It was a ghastly and terrifying spectacle for those with stomach enough to look, and not so much as a cloth to cover the crucified's loins.

Ghastlier still was when the soldiers, whatever their reasons, decided to end the suffering by breaking the legs of those on the crosses. No longer able to push up far enough to unburden the lungs and draw air, the condemned suffocated quickly.

Jesus did not last so long as that. When the soldiers came to break His legs—it was nearly sundown and both the Sabbath and Passover were about to begin and the priests did not want this unfinished business to defile the day—Jesus was already dead. The scourging, the loss of blood and hope, broke Him before the soldiers could do that last, undignified work on His legs. Surely His surrender had something to do with it: He did not fight death, did not fight for His life. He prayed for those who abused Him, blessed those who cursed Him, forgave those who pierced Him, and then He died. He had lived only a few hours, His weakness and strength perfectly, if gruesomely, joined.

His disciples had fled by then, most of them, doubly afraid: They did not want to see, did not want to be seen. They were terrified of what God might do in terrible wrath against those who killed Jesus, and perhaps they were more afraid that God would do nothing. That this was the end.

Jesus' only company at the last were two criminals flanking Him left and right, one at each side in His ironic glory.[48] One of them seems to have joined with Jesus' accusers to deride Him, although we cannot be sure if the man's words were mocking or pleading, a feeble attempt to anesthetize his own suffering by torturing Jesus, or a prayer, half-hoped words when that was all the hope he had left, born of something approaching faith. "Are you not the Christ? Save yourself and us!"[49] Perhaps he wanted to believe that Jesus could do such a thing, was such a One.

Jesus could not do what this man asked, any more than He could have made bread in the wilderness or let Peter walk on water. Jesus could not come down, could not save Himself or the malefactor or the other criminal or anyone else for that matter, at least not in the way the man demanded Him to. Jesus could not answer the malefactor's tortured prayer any more than God could answer Jesus' prayer in Gethsemane. And like that night in the garden, just the night before and so long ago, after Jesus' anguished petition there was only silence. And heartbreak. This cup of suffering and death would not pass from any of them.

The other thief's fear and faith was different, as if he somehow knew that Jesus' suffering too was different. He chided his fellow criminal—"Have you no fear of God?" he barked, here now at the last when you will soon see Him? "We suffer justly for our crimes, but this man is innocent." And then, looking to Jesus, said,

"Remember me when you come into your kingdom."

"Today you will be with me in Paradise,"[50] Jesus replied.

It was a moment like no other in all the history of the world. There are some who have suggested that, were they able somehow to be one character in all the New Testament, they would choose him—the "good thief"—who both died with Jesus and shared with Him the last conversation Jesus ever had earthly breath to join.[51] If Jesus died *for* both of those crucified with Him, indeed for all those on Golgotha's hillside that day—for the ones who had fled, for the Romans and the Jews, the tax collectors and the sinners, the living and the dead and the ones not yet born—He died *with* the one who blessed Him in His agony.

We too suffer justly for our sins; so many times that is the case. We fear admitting it, confessing it. We fight against the unavoidable truth that we too are powerless. We see ourselves isolated, imagine that only we know what it is to be cut off, separated as we pray our agonized prayers. We are afraid we don't understand, or that we do. The good we want to do we do not, as Paul said it, and the very thing we try not to do we do over and over again.[52] We are scared to be alone, scared to be with others. We are afraid of intimacy and of separation. We are scared of so many things, and sometimes we are afraid that being with Jesus only makes it worse, for there is a cross and nails, and all around us unloving people to love and unmerciful people to forgive. But there is something else too—intimacy, fellowship, shared suffering—if we follow. Where Jesus is, there we are too.

During Holy Week I encourage the members of our church to wear a cross—not like the ones with which we bejewel our fashions, but something more stark, large, obvious. If crosses are not untypical jewelry, most people wear them as accent, not a symbol of Jesus' suffering, but a fashion statement.

I invite us to make a different kind of statement, a sign of our always and absolute devotion, or at least as absolute as our devotion can be, for at least these last days of Lent. We drape Jesus' suffering around our necks, an outward and visible sign of an inward and spiritual determination to love whom He loves and serve whom He serves, to follow where He leads and die with Him too, should it come to that. We are pledged to Jesus, vow to give what is asked of us even if that means our lives.

We put on the crosses routinely in these days, but we do not wear them casually. Day by day we try to recall the full significance of this small act, and Holy Week by Holy Week the meaning is more and more clear. We give ourselves to be crucified with Jesus. We keep His death ever before us and pledge our own. We wear our crosses and make our sacrifices that our lives might become cruciform.

We stretch out our arms to the world. It can be a fearful posture, unfailingly uncomfortable, to shape ourselves after the pattern of a cross. It is not a natural pose. One has to work at it, exercise, build the strength, and quell the anguish. No one wants to die; everyone fears a ghastly death. But to save our life or keep it pristine is to lose it altogether, and that kind of cowardice proves a death more ghastly still.

We take up our crosses daily, surrender ourselves to what may come from following Jesus, knowing that to die without Him is death indeed. And day by day Jesus chooses to bring His cross to where we are, to be with us. Where His servants are, there He is too,[53] to suffer and die with us so that we do not have to die alone.

His presence gives us strength to live His life, to die our death. His presence does not palliate our pain or alter our circumstance, nor, usually, does our surrender. But His presence with us, if we are mindful of it, can make even the most fearful of moments, the most barren of wildernesses, the harshest of crosses, a place of conversation and intimacy, a place of friendship with Jesus.

Affirmation: Jesus comes as Suffering Servant.

Confession: We are afraid of His suffering and afraid of our own for His sake.

Discipleship Task: To comprehend the message of His suffering and death as central, not accidental, to His mission and to follow Jesus by moving from fear to surrender.

Easter [Middle English *estre*, from Old English *ēastre*; akin to Old High German *ōstarun* (plural) Easter, Old English *ēast* east] : a feast that commemorates Christ's resurrection and is observed with variations of date due to different calendars on the first Sunday after the paschal full moon

Chapter 6

From Skepticism to Belief

Easter Day and Season

Long before the postmodernists vanquished the Enlightenment chimera of unlensed seeing and ungrounded truth, [Flannery] O'Connor knew her faith to be the basis of her vision. "It is popular," she observed, "to believe that in order to see clearly one must believe nothing." The true order, as she discerned, is the other way around.

— Ralph C. Wood

A monastery follows the liturgical year, the great cycles of Advent, Christmas, Lent and Easter, as well as the calm flow of Ordinary Time. From the repetition of saints' days, feasts, and solemnities over the course of a lifetime, a Christian monastic seeks to experience what Paul Philibert has described . . . as "the mystery of our living between two worlds, one of space and time, the other of promise and expectation."

— Kathleen Norris

Men can heal the lustful. Angels can heal the malicious. Only God can heal the proud.

— John Climacus

D o you not remember?"
      That is what the bedazzling messengers asked the bedazzled women — Mary Magdalene, Joanna, and the other Mary (Jesus' mother? Lazarus's sister?), and some other women besides. The question rattled the dark and empty tomb into which the women had gone looking for the ruined body of their crucified friend. They had come with burial spices, expecting to see nothing other than death, to smell nothing other than stench, to feel nothing other than a fresh wave of grief when they got to the spot where He was buried and opened the grave.

But when they went into the grave they found . . . cloths. Nothing else.

Only then there was a figure in dazzling white, or was it two, or was it a multitude of the heavenly host praising God and filling the empty darkness with dazzling light, as they had that night in Bethlehem? "Do you not remember?" asked the messengers, but how could the women remember with such grief in their hearts, such a light in their eyes? Why would they want to? It hurt too much, remembering all that their friend, their teacher, their Lord had been through. Grief buried recollection.

The women were doing their duty, going through the motions, coming to the tomb to embalm their friend, barely thinking as they did, and never thinking to hope. There was nothing *to* hope. Not yet.

The sun was not yet up when the women came to the tomb. They navigated their way by the first glimmers of dawn. They could barely see when they entered, their eyes were so accustomed to the darkness. Suddenly the light of angels flashed before them, and they were frightened with a new kind of fear.

"Do you not *believe* what He told you?" Yes, they believed, some things anyway. Unlike the Sadducees, these women believed in the "last day," when all the righteous would rise again.[1] Reunion and vindication would come, but way in the future and everyone together. Almost nothing in the women's experience or learning prepared them to hope for anything else, to expect anything at the tomb other than death and grief and darkness.

Of course, they had seen how Jesus had given life back to Lazarus,[2] to a little girl,[3] to a young man,[4] but all those would die again. The women could not have hoped, after what they had seen on Friday afternoon, would not have wished for Jesus to live again if He were going to have to die again.

"Do you not believe what He told you?" The question pounded in the women's temples, and they searched their memories for something Jesus had said to make sense of this light and these cloths and the empty tomb. For a long moment Jesus' words of hope or promise were as buried as their friend. Then all at once something vague began to take shape, Jesus' words that the angels wanted them to remember, from way back in Galilee: "The Son of Man must be handed over to sinners and be crucified and on the third day *rise again*."[5]

Yes, of course, *now* they remembered how Jesus said there would be betrayal and suffering and death, but that death would not have the final word. "I am the resurrection and the life"[6] — they remembered Him saying that too. What they could not remember was what, exactly, they thought He had meant when He said these words, or what He seemed to want them to think.

Is *this* what He was telling them? That He *Himself* would rise again? Is that what He meant?

Who *could* believe in such a thing? Nothing in life or

experience prepares anyone to believe it. No wonder the rest of the disciples did not believe the news when the women told them what they had seen and heard.

The Crucifixion proved centrifugal for those who loved Jesus. The force of His death shattered them, distanced them, drove them away from each other—geographically and otherwise. With all that had happened, they no longer trusted each other entirely and perhaps not at all, for promises to Jesus had been made and broken. Protestations of allegiance had evaporated by courtyard fires. Friends had betrayed one another into the hands of merciless men, and fear had gripped them all. Now there was doubt. Wariness. Skepticism.

The women came back early on the first day of the week, telling of an empty tomb. At least two of the disciples went to check out the women's story—yes, they agreed, the tomb was empty,[7] but that was all they agreed on. The women reported they had seen angels, and Mary Magdalene said she had seen the Lord Himself, but the other disciples considered it an idle tale, a rumor, wishful thinking.[8]

"Do you not remember what He said?" the women asked the men, full now with both memory and understanding. The men could not remember or, if they did remember, could not believe that this is what Jesus had taught them. Their skepticism was double-edged; they doubted both the women's Easter morning testimony, and they doubted Jesus' teaching.

Maybe they just couldn't let themselves see beyond the obvious, the tangible. They were fishermen, after all, tax collectors and practical men used to holding in their hands dead fish and cold coins and hard truth. They traded in realities, tendered in common sense, had to have proof of things. Until they saw Jesus with their own eyes, touched Him with their own hands, they would not, could not believe. *Would that it were true*, they might have thought. *I wish it were. But this is the real world. Things like that do not happen.*

Mr. Roberts was the former lay leader at a church I served, but he didn't believe what I or any other preacher preached there. He told me as much over lunch soon after I arrived. He said he supported the Church, gave to the Church, even led the Church because the Church served as guarantor of our society's best values—morality, democracy, character, and generosity. I had already noticed that at the end of each Sunday's service, as the congregation with one voice enumerated its beliefs by means of the Apostles' Creed, Mr. Roberts said not a word beyond "I believe in God. . . ." If I happened to be looking his way, he rather ceremoniously shut his mouth, pursed his lips, as the rest of us continued on.

He did believe in God, he said, but in his own way—after his own image and likeness, he joked. He did not believe much else, found ample reason for skepticism in the sciences. He had written a book, he told me, published it himself and sold every last copy at the local bookstore, wherein he catalogued and buttressed his rejections of the received traditions. No one of sound, modern mind, for example, could believe in the virginal conception of Jesus. Such a teaching violated the established laws of biology. And no one could believe in the stories of Jesus' miracles either, because they were written in a prescientific era when "miracle" meant only an unusual or, at that particular moment, inexplicable occurrence. Now, he said—in these days—we can explain with medical certainty such things as "demon possession" (epilepsy) or even Lazarus's death (a catatonic state), and we can disprove with equal certainty many of the cosmological assumptions of the Bible.

The Gospels were unreliable too, unabashed propaganda and full of contradictions besides. No sensible person could honestly believe in the Resurrection, he said—that, especially. "Dead is dead," he told me. Flesh cannot be regenerated, and neither Baron von Frankenstein nor the Lord God Almighty could bring the dead back to life. Wishful thinking, he said, shaking his head slightly and sipping his tea.

I had never before known anyone within the Church who so boldly denounced the basic tenets of the gospel (though I have run into a few more since then). I suspected, however, that many Christians crossed their fingers at the same articles of the Creed that Mr. Roberts rejected. I knew some Christians were of "two minds," seeing the world in one way on the weekends and in another in between—and preachers, sadly, among them.

Some stay stuck in the gap, God knows, unable to either believe entirely or doubt completely. But Jesus takes pity on us time after time and comes to us, shows Himself alive among us. When He does, the proud fortress of our doubt crumbles, and in its ruined place there remains only humility and thanks—the benefits of knowing, believing, truly seeing what we could never otherwise have imagined as true.

On Easter evening, the disciples were gathered in the Upper Room; only Thomas was not there. Jesus appeared to the rest of them, blessed them and breathed on them, and in that moment they believed what Mary had been telling them since first light. When those who had seen Jesus told Thomas that Jesus was alive, the disciple was as skeptical of their word as they had been of Mary's. "Unless I see for myself," he said, "unless I can touch the wounds, unless Jesus Himself proves it to me, I will not believe."

The next week they gathered together again, and this time Thomas was there. Jesus appeared and went straight toward him: "See! Touch! Believe!" Jesus said. "Do not doubt."

And Thomas believed.[9]

Thomas is indeed the twin brother of us all, not only of Mr. Roberts whose skepticism was so obvious, but also of the rest of us whose head and heart are too dramatically divorced. We say the words, most of us, but sometimes wink as we do and do not always believe all of what we are saying—our own little skepticisms leaking into our prayers and professions—or at least we do not always believe that, even if it is true, it makes any real difference in the real world.

Nothing in our experience, in our world, prepares us for this announcement of Resurrection—that, especially. But Jesus comes, shows Himself both wounded and alive in His Word, in the sacraments, in the peace that passes understanding. He is not angry—He remembers we are dust—but offers to us the invitation to know beyond the verifiable facts, to trust beyond our reasonable doubts, to live beyond the strictures and ravages of time. "Do not doubt but believe," He says.

Easter by Easter, in my part of the world, at least, believers get up while the sun is still beyond the eastern horizon to stand shivering with our sleepy-eyed friends in the chill of a church cemetery, new candles in hand. Preachers and texts and sometimes even trumpets prompt us to memory and proclamation. "Do you not remember?" some white-robed someone will say, an angel or maybe the preacher. "Christ is risen!"

"The Lord is risen indeed!" we the people respond with quavering voice. We do remember, and we want to believe.

With Scriptures and hymns, music and flame, we gather ourselves and our voices to the ancient choruses and recite while it is still mostly dark the heart of our faith: how Jesus "was crucified, dead and buried," but "on the third day he rose from the dead." On these fourteen words hang the whole of Christian history, the hopes of all the faithful, the future of the entire world.

Death is not the final word, for any of us, for the world itself. That is what we say, what we sing and preach — and we really want to believe it, though sometimes we say what we say and sing what we sing with our fingers crossed. We are in the cemetery, after all, and no one is yet coming up out of the grave. Jesus did, we say, we believe, we wish, we hope, but what might that even *begin* to look like?

We are practical people, "real world" people, where cancer is often stronger than our prayers for a loved one's healing. Yes, sometimes, there are reprieves and curings, and we bandy the word *miracle* about, but our loved ones will die again, all of them. We will die too, and the miracles are rare when they come.

It may be an idle tale, an opiate, this message of the Resurrection. Still we want to believe it, at least with one part of ourselves. We really do want to believe it. With passing years most of us pray that our skepticism dissipates with other relics of arrogant youth. We gradually realize that we do not know as much as we flattered ourselves to think. There is far more going on in the world than even the sharpest of young eyes can take in, and by grace older, dimmer eyes see that our only hope for life and death is founded in God, that God's goodness is stronger than the world's evil and its most powerful servant — death.

So we stand in the cemetery as dawn kisses the headstones. Moment by moment the blushing granite markers reveal the men, women, children whose names are carved deep into the stone. We are surrounded by the young and the old, who died sudden, tragic death or long, lingering death. Many unjustly, unhappily, unfulfilled, and before or after their time. As the sun continues to rise, we begin to sing and remember and proclaim and believe that death cannot have the last word. It must not and will not, and that is worth believing this morning and every other.

That, more than any other reason, is why we continue to gather with our cold, sleepy friends to join the song begun by Christians in time zones east and untold generations past, to carry the song to time zones west and unknown generations to come, that He is not here but risen.

We say it faithfully until we can know it entirely—Christ is risen indeed!—and that may not be until after we ourselves have been buried in a place like this. But by grace we believe, and believe it more and more, faith following praise.

We remember. We believe. Most of us first approach the story with our heads—how can it be true? Dead is dead. Sunday by Sunday, Easter by Easter, and death by precious death, we come with the women at first light of dawn and find that in our hearts, finally, we begin to trust in what should be true, what ought to be true.

Yes, we believe in what we have not yet seen, what cannot yet be proven. Lord, help our unbelief. We confess that we are skeptics as well as disciples, but disciples more than skeptics because we rise to proclaim what we have not experienced, not in its fullness. We gather to sing and provoke each other to believe and remember that although Jesus was dead, He is alive again and that we, though mortal as He, shall one day share His immortality.

Shivering for all sorts of reasons, we hear again the curious stories of the women and the angels and the empty tomb. Our bodies shiver; our voices break. If it is *true*, all that the women tell Jesus' followers then and now—that the tomb is empty and there are angels afoot—then there is ample reason for our cemeteries and churches to be full Easter Sunday by Easter Sunday.

If, on the other hand, the tomb is not empty, then our faith and our preaching, our worship and our hearts surely are. Paul said it all:

> If Christ has not been raised, then our preaching has been in vain and your faith is in vain. And we are even guilty of lying, of blasphemy, of misrepresenting God, if we testify that God raised Jesus from the dead if in fact He did not. If Christ is not raised, then our preaching and your faith are futile, pointless, absurd, and we are still in our sins. Just as surely, those who have died in Christ are gone. If Christ has not been raised, we are of all people most to be pitied—the world's most pathetic and wretched.[10]

The last sentence of that text always frightens me a little: "If Christ has not been raised, we are of all people most to be pitied." Paul put all his eggs, as William Sloane Coffin once suggested, in one Easter basket.

There were many in those Corinthian days (when the Church was still young) who claimed that the Resurrection was not true, just as there are today (when the Church has been around long enough to develop a fierce opposition). They said it was but a tale, a metaphor at most, an understandable but ultimately deplorable fiction crafted by the desolate disciples and sold to unsophisticated and death-fearing masses.

Folks say the same to us these days, and more: The women went to the wrong garden or the wrong tomb, that Jesus' body decayed rapidly, or that it was eaten by wild dogs. Some early believers contended there was no body at all, never had been, that Jesus was a spiritual being who only appeared to be human.

And "pity us," Paul said, if the skeptics are right, if pity is something skeptics and unbelieving sophisticates can muster. If Jesus has not been raised, those of us who follow Him, who name Him and claim Him as Lord, are of all people the most deluded. We have staked our lives and future on a lie, have trusted our souls to absurdity, have hoped in what is not true and will die wretched, hopeless deaths.

Pity us if Christ has not been raised.

But what if Christ has been raised? If mourning has broken, who to pity then?

If I had been Jesus and I had been raised from the dead, I think I might have paid an early Easter morning visit to Herod or Pilate. To Annas or Caiaphas. To the centurion with the flagellum or the other ones with the hammers and spears. I may have asked for my robe back, first, just to see the look on their faces.

Then I might have gone to see my disciples, see their shock, ask why they were surprised. Weren't they listening? After that I might have taught them a little rap with a straightforward message for all those who had spit on me and cursed me, ridiculed me and rejoiced in my destruction: "The Lord is back and there's gonna be trouble, hey na, hey na, the Lord is back!"

Of course, that was not what happened, not what Jesus did, not what the disciples learned or preached. Jesus had prayed from the cross, "Father, forgive them; they do not know what they are doing," and after the Resurrection He practiced what He had prayed. He forgave Thomas, who doubted. He forgave Peter, who denied Him and ran away. He would, I believe, have forgiven Judas to his face as He surely did from His heart.

No surprise then that the forgiven disciples preached the Resurrection as itself a kind of forgiveness. "You too acted in ignorance," Peter told those gathered in Jerusalem for Pentecost. "Turn now to this One you rejected and find forgiveness. Believe in this One whom you killed and find life. Turn to this One you despised and find love, this One you did not know and find that He knows you and gave Himself for you."[11]

If Christ be not raised, the "real world" really is as lost as most days it appears to be. The seven deadly sins become the habits of highly effective people. But if Christ is raised, we are of all people most blessed.

We will not fear sickness or death or grieve hopelessly when our loved ones die. We will find a peace that passes understanding and a community of faith that helps make peace in the world. We will face each day with strength and hope, a serenity not based on mere circumstance. We will know the bankruptcy of power for power's sake, of beauty for seduction's sake, of money for self-determination's sake, and we will trade in a different currency —humility, service, vulnerability.

We will not fear though Heaven and earth should shake, for God alone is eternal and the Resurrection proves it. We will be quick to forgive even those who abuse us, to pray for those who malign us, to share the hope of the Resurrection even with those who consider it an idle tale, wishful thinking. We will remember all Jesus has said, all Jesus has done, and we will say and do likewise, a bit at a time, till we see Him as He is, till we are like Him at last. We will believe what we have heard.

Long after I had moved to another church and then to another, Mr. Roberts died. As he lay in the hospital, he was very much alone, I am told, isolated in his denials. His skepticism had hardened into bitterness, sad to say. I am told he refused to see his wife or his children in the last days before his death and, not surprisingly, would not consider a visit from the current minister of the church. He barked at the doctors, the nurses, growled his wishlessness toward the ceiling of his room.

He had believed little. He had hoped even less. He died a sad and angry old man.

But God is merciful—His property, as the old prayer reminds us, is always to have compassion. It is my own prayer that Jesus came to His embittered, disbelieving child in much the same way He went to Thomas that Easter evening so long ago.

"See!" He said to Mr. Roberts. "Touch! Do not doubt but believe! Live," He said, "as I myself am alive!" And I choose to believe that Mr. Roberts does.

Affirmation: Jesus comes as resurrected Lord.

Confession: We are skeptical as to the meaning or import of Resurrection.

Discipleship Task: To hear again the message of the women and angels and to follow Jesus by moving from skepticism to belief.

Pentecost [Middle English, from Old English *pentecosten*, from Late Latin *pentecoste*, from Greek *pentēkostē*, literally, fiftieth day, from *pentēkostos* fiftieth, from *pentēkonta* fifty, from *penta-* + *-konta* (akin to Latin *viginti* twenty)] **1:** *Shabuoth* [Hebrew *shābhū'ōth*, literally, weeks]: a Jewish holiday observed on the sixth and seventh of Sivan in commemoration of the revelation of the Ten Commandments at Mt. Sinai—called also *Pentecost* **2:** a Christian feast on the seventh Sunday after Easter commemorating the descent of the Holy Spirit on the apostles—called also *Whitsunday*

Chapter 7

From Waiting to Witness

Pentecost

The Spirit works where he *wills*. . . . God's Spirit does not blow when he *must*, but only when he *wills*.

— Hans Küng

Everything that seems empty is full of the angels of God.

— Saint Hilary

An important aspect of [prayer] . . . has been described as "attentive waiting." I think it's also a fair description of the writing process. Once, when I was asked, "What is the main thing a poet does?" I was inspired to answer, "We wait." A spark is struck; an event inscribed with a message — this is important, pay attention — and a poet scatters a few words like seeds in a notebook. Months or even years later, those words bear fruit.

— Kathleen Norris

Pentecost did not, as it is sometimes portrayed, begin with noise—the rush as of a violent wind, the clash of overlapping languages, or even the crackle of cloven tongues as of fire. Pentecost came to all of that, to be sure, but it did not begin there.

It began instead in silence.

The power of Pentecost was not the preaching of Peter or the witnessing done by the other disciples or even human words at all, though there will be power in all of that. The power of Pentecost was in the disciples' waiting and prayer.

The initial movement of Pentecost was not the coming of the Holy Spirit but rather the going, the Ascension, of Jesus.

For a moment His disciples just stood there, chins in the air and hearts in their throat, looking up into the sky, to the cloud where Jesus had vanished.[1] Who could blame them? More than once over the last few weeks Jesus had disappeared, left them alone, only to rejoin them later. First He had been taken from them forcefully—He was crucified, dead, and buried—and then He was alive, miraculously with His disciples again, back in their barricaded Upper Room.[2] Over and over He disappeared mysteriously only to startle and sometimes terrify them by reappearing or materializing once more.

Easter afternoon, incognito with two of His disciples—they did not recognize so much as His voice—but suddenly He was apparent to them in the breaking of bread. But then, as quickly as they had eyes open enough to see Him, He left them again.[3]

Later that night, all of the disciples were together in Jerusalem sharing their stories of how they had seen Him—and suddenly He was with them all, to their delight and horror and wonder.[4]

Early one morning, some time later, Jesus came to the shore of Galilee's sea where a few of His disciples—Simon, Thomas, Nathaniel, James and John, and one more besides—had gone fishing. The erstwhile and feckless fishermen were still in the boat after a long, tiring night of hauling empty nets from the water, when suddenly, at Jesus' word (though at first they did not know it was Jesus), they had more fish than they could haul in. By the time they made it back to shore to see Him (they now knew who the stranger was), Jesus had made them a fresh breakfast.

Luke tells us—and it is a tantalizing phrase, intriguing, even—that after Easter Jesus "presented himself alive to [the disciples] by many convincing proofs."[5] Some of them apparently needed convincing, for, as Matthew writes, when the disciples met the resurrected Christ on a hillside in Galilee, many believed and worshiped, but "some doubted."[6] Sadly, Luke does not tell us what those convincing proofs were, but we know that for forty days He appeared here and there, now and then, sometimes passing through walls and sometimes eating fish, showing His scars, giving the disciples instruction, breathing His breath like peace onto them.

The disciples who did believe surely began to look over their shoulders, glance out the corners of their eyes, listen for the first soft rustlings of curtains or birdsong twitter that might prove a harbinger of Jesus' appearing. Who knew on what dark morning or distant shore, in what bright dream or familiar haunt, Jesus would return with instructions and counsel and benediction?

The morning of the Ascension—forty days after Easter morning—Jesus led His disciples out as far as Bethany, the same little town where Mary had anointed Him. There He anointed His disciples with a promise of power and blessing and peace. "You will receive power when the Holy Spirit has come upon you; and you will be my witnesses in Jerusalem, in all Judea and Samaria, and to the ends of the earth."[7] But "stay here in the city until you have been clothed with power from on high,"[8] Jesus said. Wait in the city, for the "Promise of My Father."[9] Wait.

Right after that, as they were watching, He was lifted up. A cloud took Him out of their sight. Did they know that this was their last glimpse of Him? Perhaps the disciples stood looking up into the sky because they did not know but what Jesus might appear yet again, and this time they wanted to be ready. Or maybe they knew, deep down, that this time He was gone, that they would not see Him again till they too, one way or another, were carried away to join Him.

Into that empty moment came two angels in white robes, appearing much as they had to the women at the tomb and as an angel had appeared long before that to the old priest, the young virgin, and to Joseph. Angels had appeared in the Bethlehem sky too, filling each empty place and heart and situation with surprising praise, remembrance, and command. This time, as the disciples looked up, the angels said, "Chins and noses down! Yes, He will appear again. Yes, you will see Him again. But not today. Now go, do as He has said."

Friedrich Nietzsche, patron antisaint of all who curse the Church and its Christ, once said to the faithful of his day something wise: "You will have to look more redeemed for me to believe in your Redeemer."

Perhaps it was only malediction. Might it have also been invitation? How can we look more redeemed? What might we offer as convincing proof that Christ is alive among us?

We might offer as evidence that we feed the hungry or clothe the naked. We visit the widow and orphan, and we love one another. We grant friendship to the rejected and radical hospitality to exiles. We take note of those who are beaten and abandoned by the roadside, and we make like the Samaritan, go and do likewise. We witness to the once and abiding life of Jesus by obeying His commands, by living as He showed us, by speaking faithful words too.

We offer our testimony, our words. We witness, we teach, we preach and even write. We offer our voices, our convictions, in the public square and pray to be heard for our truthful and persuasive speaking, our eloquent apology, our insight.

Yes, yes. But the last instruction Jesus ever gave His disciples was something other than any of what we sometimes point to as proof. "Wait," Jesus said. Wait.

He did not tell them to go but to stay in Jerusalem. He did not tell them to do but to sit. He did not tell them to preach, not yet, but to pray. There will be time for more active work later, He as much as said, but the first work, for now, is to sit, to wait for the promise of the Father.

"This," He said, "is what you have heard from me; for John baptized with water, but you will be baptized with the Holy Spirit not many days from now."[10] "You will be my witnesses," Jesus said, "in Jerusalem, in all Judea and Samaria, and to the ends of the earth."[11] His words are command and promise, both at once. But *wait*. That first. "As yet you lack power. As yet you do not know what *to* say. The Holy Spirit will bring you to remembrance of all that I have said, but you do not yet remember enough. Before you can speak, you must hear. Before you hear, you must wait."

So the disciples returned to Jerusalem, gathered themselves together with other of their friends and Jesus' followers. Mary, the mother of Jesus, soon joined them and the other Mary did too, and together they began praying. *Together* they devoted themselves to prayer.[12] There was much to talk about, of course, but there would be time for talking later.

For now they were waiting. Silent. At prayer. Those were the first sounds of Pentecost, the first movements of their ministry, the first evidence offered to their redemption. Obedience and patience, prayer and waiting—and we can only surmise that the Holy Spirit was bringing to their remembrance some of the things Jesus had said and done.

Once, years before, on their way back from a short vacation at the beach in Tyre, Jesus and the disciples passed through an area known as the Decapolis, or "ten cities."[13] As Jesus walked along, some people came to Him, begging Him to heal their friend who was both deaf and mute.

The man could not have heard about Jesus—he did not have ears to hear—and he could not have spoken for himself to Jesus if he had. He was powerless, but Jesus was not. Jesus took him aside, spit in His hands (*ptu* is the Greek root for the word translated into English as *spit*), and then rubbed the spit on the man's tongue and stuck His spitty fingers in the man's ears. The entire episode is so earthy and physical that it unsettles us a bit (and John too, apparently, for though in his gospel Jesus does spit one time it is only on the ground to make a mud paste, a poultice, to apply neatly, as at a day spa, to a blind man's eyes[14]). In Mark's account, Jesus is *Peanuts'* Pigpen, spitting and rubbing, making a holy and healing mess.

Jesus speaks, and suddenly the man can hear. Jesus touches the man's tongue, and now the man can speak plainly. He is no longer silent in what had seemed to him a silent world; by the gift of God he has power to speak.

The miracle is a picture of Pentecost. Jesus promised that the Spirit would come and touch the disciples, ears and tongues, to help them hear and remember all that He said and did, to make them strong to preach all they had seen and known. And so they waited, prayed for themselves and their friends that the Spirit would work just such a miracle as that.

And at Pentecost the Holy Spirit did.

Another Sunday down . . . I wonder how many more to go.

I ask myself this question some Sundays even before I finish shaking hands. And then, as I walk back down the center aisle to gather my things — my hymnal and Bible, my bulletin and manuscript — the self-interrogation intensifies. Did I say today what needed saying? Did I speak the gospel? Did I do justice to the text, to the human condition? Did I preach both the need for repentance and the gift of forgiveness?

And this: If what I just preached were my last sermon (and one of these days, somewhere along the line, a sermon I preach will in fact be my last one), would it be a fitting end for my ministry? Would I be content for that to be my last word on the matter of God's way with the world and with us?

In some ways the first few moments after morning worship are such a sweet, placid relief. The week's study and prayer, whether lots of it or little, have found some kind of expression. Even before preaching I have taught a Church school class — my faith twice delivered to the saints. Now I can sit down, rest my voice, ice my knee. There are 166 hours before I have to do it all again. Only 166, but 166!

In other ways the first few moments after morning worship are the hardest of the week. The questions are like boulders under the surface of the calm pond. I think back over the morning and invariably wish I had taken a couple of more hours for silence — to study a bit more, to read another chapter or two, to pray harder. Maybe if I had written a couple of more drafts, sharpened my similes and polished my metaphors, the sermon would have been better, more effective and winsome.

Most Sundays I walk back down the aisle and shake my head

grimly, knowing in my heart of hearts that yet again I did not say all I might have, did not preach either bravely or persuasively enough, did not do justice either to the text or its Lord. So please, God, give me at least one more chance to do it right, to make this next Sunday's effort a fitting "last" one should it come to that.

Next Sunday's sermon, if there is to be one, begins with this silence, this understanding that I have neither the power nor the knowledge to be the kind of witness I am called to be. All of our witness, however it is that we witness — going, doing, serving, sharing — all of it begins in the awareness that we cannot do all of what needs to be done, cannot prove our faith, cannot save the world or its needy children. We must admit that we who pray for the conversion of the world are ourselves in constant need of converting.[15]

"Let not many of you become teachers," the brother of our Lord said wisely,[16] and he might have said, "Let not many of you invoke Jesus as the reason for your work — for all who do so, whatever they do, will 'be judged with the greater strictness.'" By Nietzsche and by many others.

That verse is branded on my brain. I will be judged with greater strictness — and maybe that is why my hands are always so cold after I preach and teach. They are most likely cold with fear of teaching incorrectly or preaching insufficiently, of leading God's people astray. I do not know enough. Cannot remember enough. Cannot adequately share what little I do know and remember. God, I know it to be true.

I need the touch of Jesus before I can even begin to offer Jesus to others. There must be silence before there is speech, humble waiting before there is bold witness.

All of us who would witness, however it is we witness, begin with the confession that we are powerless. Without Jesus, without His touch, without the coming of the Holy Spirit to fire our work, we are sound and shallow fervor availing nothing.

But always—and if this were not so we could not, I think, go on—always, that bleak sense of failure and inadequacy, the awareness of another missed opportunity, dissipates into a warm awareness of God's prevailing mercy and grace. God knew just what He was getting when He called us. Jesus had no illusions about the disciples, and we must have no illusions about ourselves. Those of us who name the Name and claim His ministry do so in the full awareness that we cannot in our own power demonstrate Him alive to those who will not believe it, cannot offer convincing proof other than our selves, our common life and work—and those shot through with pride and prejudice.

There are many gaps, gaping holes in our lives and witness, but God has called us, and I have to believe God is prepared to fill with His own Spirit what is lacking in us—if we but wait.

If we do not, if we rush to our work—just go and do—we go naked, unclothed by the promise and presence of God. But if we wait, speak when spoken to, tell only what we are given to remember and know, go and do as we have been commanded, we may find we are indeed witnesses almost in spite of ourselves.

I wonder who was more surprised that day in Jerusalem: the crowds who heard Peter, or Peter himself? He who on the night of Jesus' trial had been unable to admit to a slave girl that he even knew Jesus preaches to many thousands, and several thousand of them are converted on the spot. There is a rush to salvation after fiery preaching, fiery preaching after the coming of the Holy Spirit in power, power that came to the disciples as they waited.

"Of course we are weak," admitted Ghislain Lafont, a French Benedictine who was lecturing to a group of mostly younger monks, "unable to cope. But if we can maintain faith, hope and charity, it will radiate somehow. And people who come to us may find in us what we can no longer see in ourselves."[17]

By the time I make it to my office, I bask in the humble awareness that my last sermon, whenever it is, is not *the* last sermon—which is to say, not God's last sermon. However many Sundays I have left, God has *all* of them left, and whatever I do not say will get said sometime, by someone. It is not my gospel, after all. God will keep on preaching, filling in gaps, long after I stop. God *won't* stop till everyone hears at last and believes.

Cold hands? Yes, but a warm heart too. Strangely warmed. I *love* Sunday afternoons.

Affirmation: Jesus sends the empowering and vocalizing Spirit.

Confession: We are eager to speak and reluctant to wait, so our words and our witness avail nothing.

Discipleship Task: To wait and pray for the power God offers us, and then to follow Jesus by moving from waiting to witness, from prayer to ministry, from silence to speech.

Trinity [Middle English *trinite*, from Anglo-French *trinité*, from Late Latin *trinitat-*, *trinitas* state of being threefold, from Latin *trinus* three-fold] **1:** the unity of Father, Son, and Holy Spirit as three persons in one Godhead according to Christian dogma **3:** the Sunday after Whitsunday observed as a feast in honor of the Trinity

Chapter 8

From Familiarity to Mystery

Trinity Sunday

I remember a visit to the ruins of the Fountains Abbey in Yorkshire, when, as we walked from one part of the site to the other, a friend read the relevant text for the official guide at each point. When we reached the ruins of the Chapter House, the text was as follows: "Here the monks gathered every Sunday to hear a sermon from the Abbot, except on Trinity Sunday, owing to the difficulty of the subject."

— LESLIE NEWBIGIN

"Safe?" said Mr. Beaver. "Don't you hear what Mrs. Beaver tells you? Who said anything about safe? 'Course he isn't safe. But he's good. He's the King, I tell you."

— C. S. LEWIS

I can still remember walking home from Crieve Hall Elementary School, stepping through the back door to see that a remarkable transformation had occurred since that morning. In our back den, the hub and hive of all things in our family, the furniture had been moved out and replaced by a great wooden frame—a couple of sawhorses and long side beams that must have been five or six feet long. White fabric was stretched across the frame, a kind of sandwich, really, with a layer of linen on top and another beneath, separated by a padding of cotton. It was a quilting rack, of course.

I can still remember the way my pulse would quicken. If there was a quilting rack in the den it meant my grandmother's sisters were there too. Memie, my grandmother, lived to be 104 and a week. My favorite of the sisters was the oldest one, Nanny, who was elegant and funny. Cokie, the youngest, looked and acted the oldest. She had the sourest expression and grunted with her every step. But Cokie—we sometimes called her Pokey because she moved so slowly—made the best blackberry jam cakes in the history of the world.

The cakes came out of the oven to be slathered with some kind of sugary icing, and there was *nothing* pokey about the way we went for our forks and dug in, sometimes without even slicing the cake first. We just ate it whole, right off the plate. Nanny and Memie tried in vain to duplicate the recipe Cokie gave them. Mom tried to duplicate *their* recipe, but it was never the same. The sisters and nieces think Cokie held out on them, for some reason did not include a crucial ingredient or something, took the secret to her grave.

Whatever intrigue characterized the kitchen, there was none of that at the quilting rack. I loved to watch the three of them, sitting here or there, stitching awhile, intricate and delicate and amazing handiwork, sometimes talking among themselves, sometimes silent except for Cokie's grunting. One of them, or two of them, or all three as if on cue would move their chairs to start working somewhere else. It was a mysterious dance, and when they did it they too grew mysterious.

The three sisters looked different, somehow, when they quilted, their faces and posture changed by the work. They almost glowed. And sometimes they glowered too. Especially then I knew to keep my distance and hold my tongue—at least till they looked up or stopped for the day. Or maybe it was I who was changed, transfixed, watching in wonder as something wonderful took shape.

I could never tell exactly what they were doing, of course, and sometimes it looked as if they were stitching in the same places over and over again. Day after day I would come in from school to find the three of them at their work. I would check their progress, and for the longest time it looked like random stuff, haphazard patterns.

But there came a day, there always came a day, when I would come in after school and see that all of what had seemed random had been more purposeful than I could have imagined, that their movements and stitching, here and there, were not haphazard at all but part of a plan and design that my elementary-age eyes simply could not recognize.

Theirs was a craft beyond me. *They* knew what they were doing. I was only watching. *They* stitched a quilt that would keep me warm on a cold winter's night, and into that quilt they poured their years of experience and skill and love.

Sometimes when my grandmother and her two sisters were working, they would jab themselves with a needle—even experts are not immune to suffering—and on one or two of those quilts, if you know where to look, you can still see the tiniest trace of blood, evidence of their love and work.

And then, the work would be finished and the quilt rack put

away till next time—if there was one. They worked on each quilt as if it were their last, and then my aunts went home, and I would miss them till the next time when I would see the quilt rack and smell the jam cake and know that something wondrous was going on—warm, sweet graces for that day and for years to come.

On Trinity Sunday Christians proclaim the fullness of God—Father, Son, Holy Spirit in an inner life and relationship, eternally One and yet eternally distinct, one God in three persons, and three personal ways of knowing and experiencing the One eternal God—as He has *gradually* been revealed to us.

It is a mystery, this doctrine of ours—few Scriptures point to it directly[1]—and a true mystery, as Augustine said it, is something that one cannot know unless it is revealed, and even after it is known it cannot be explained. The Trinity is a mystery in just that way: known by revelation, evidenced in Creation, in salvation, and in abiding presence.

In the beginning, when there was nothing but darkness and chaos and void, God said, "Let there be light," and there was light. Only later did we realize that the Word by which God created the world was the eternal Word, the Word that would become flesh and dwell among us. John tells us, "In the beginning was the Word and the Word was with God and the Word was God; all things were created by that Word and apart from that Word nothing was made that has been made."[2]

Only later did we realize that in Creation, as the Word was being spoken, God's Spirit was moving on the face of the deep, that God's Spirit came upon the prophets that they might proclaim God's will, that God's Spirit came upon a virgin who conceived and bore a Son who was the Word made flesh.

God comes among us, stands apart from us, fills our lungs with breath—but as close as God might be in any given moment, He is yet far beyond us. Though we have seen Jesus' face and known His salvation in the sacraments and worship, He is a mystery still. Though the very image of God is imprinted on us, we find that we are strangers, that if we know God we still do not know Him whole. His ways are not our ways, after all, and His thoughts are not our thoughts.[3]

For the Hebrews, God's name was so holy it was not to be pronounced. When Jesus taught us to pray, He allowed us more familiar access to the Father. But familiarity should not lead us to presumption, for God is Spirit and we are dust. God is eternal and we are locked in time. We may know a language or two—maybe one or two more—but God understands every utterance His children make, speaks in all the languages of earth and Heaven besides. We may move the earth and feel ourselves mighty, but God made the earth and all of us from it.

God invites us to speak to Him;[4] Jesus calls us friends;[5] the Holy Spirit speaks to our spirits to tell us that we are the children of God.[6] But we dare not presume too much familiarity—though we, like Jesus' contemporaries, often do.

As Jesus went about His work in Galilee, there were many who thought they knew Him. "Is not this Joseph's son?"[7] they would say, or words to that effect. "Is this not Mary's boy?"[8] The latter was an insult, though we do not always hear it as such—one never called a Jewish male by his mother's name unless there was uncertainty, real or imagined, about the father's identity. The former was a benediction, but in both cases the assumption was made that "we know who this is." One way or the other the crowds thought, *He is one of us.*

One day Jesus was teaching near the Sea of Galilee; so many people had come to hear Him, hungry for the Word of God, that they crowded Him almost into the water. Jesus got into a boat,

Simon's, and had Simon put out a little ways from shore so He could finish the lesson. When Jesus had finished teaching, He told Simon to go to the deep water, let down his net for a big catch. Simon had been fishing all night and caught nothing—before Jesus arrived, Simon was already washing his nets, through for the day—but he did as Jesus asked, and sure enough there were so many fish in the net Simon had to have help to bring them in. When Simon and his friends got the fish into the boat, the boat began to sink.

Everyone was amazed but Simon. He was scared. He fell at Jesus' feet and said, "Go away from me, Lord, for I am a sinful man!"[9] He knew Jesus well enough to know he did not know Him at all. He knew himself well enough to be frightened in the presence of the Lord.

How different Simon is from many of us who, like the crowds in Capernaum or Nazareth, imagine that Jesus is just like us—that He thinks as we do and values what we do, that we know Him just as He is.

Trinity Sunday reminds us that for all our presumed familiarity with God, God is much more than we can manage. We know God, but we do not know God at all—His ways are not our ways nor His thoughts our thoughts. His Spirit bears witness with our spirits that we are the children of God, but children do not always or even often know their parents in their persons. They may know some of what their parents do, and certainly how their parents care for them, but they do not often know all of who their parents are. Not for long years, anyway, not without much conversation and life experience of their own.

There is mystery suffusing the familiarity. Familiarity gives way to mystery, and as we grow, who can tell which quality prevails or is more precious? On youth retreats at the beach, I often tell my students that we walk in this surf and what splashes on us is all ocean. But it is not all the ocean. We love the ocean, but we dare not presume we have mastered its depths or fail to remember that there is mystery here, and even danger.

We, like children, are left to wonder as to the fullness, the depth, the person of God. We know what God does, some of it; we have experienced God's love and care. We have been splashed with baptismal waters, and we feel the living near the edge of God's fullness. But it takes long years—longer than we are given in a lifetime—for us to more than begin to know who God is in Himself. Our elementary eyes have only gradually come to see what God has been doing all along. Only gradually have our eyes come to see who God has been all along.

On July 8, 1741, in the church at Enfield, Connecticut, a thirty-eight-year-old Puritan preacher by the name of Jonathan Edwards delivered one of the most famous, or infamous, sermons of all time, "Sinners in the Hands of an Angry God." Even nonbelievers have heard of this sermon and have read it if they went to high school and ever did their homework. "The bow of God's wrath is bent," Edwards said, apparently with no emotion,

> and the arrow made ready on the string, and justice bends the arrow at your heart, and strains the bow, and it is nothing but the mere pleasure of God, and that of an angry God, without any promise or obligation at all, that keeps the arrow one moment from being made drunk with your blood. . . . God holds you over the pit of hell, much as one holds a spider, or some loathsome insect over the fire.[10]

Edwards was a guest preacher in Enfield that day. The people were weeping and wailing, passing out right and left. The pastor kept trying to interrupt Edwards, asking, "But what of mercy? Is there no mercy?"

For Edwards, that day, maybe not. Maybe there was no mercy. The God Edwards presented was not concerned with His children's predicament but only with His own holiness. Perhaps that is why many nonbelievers point to that very sermon, or sermons like it, when they are explaining why they do not believe. They do not want to believe in a God like that, mysterious and dangerous, distant and unmerciful, do not want their faith to be fear.

Edwards lived a long time ago, of course. In many modern places among most modern people, there has been a complete shift away from his kind of theology. The pendulum has swung. If Edwards and others like him made God too foreign, too different and "other," in the long days since many other preachers (and teachers and counselors) have persuaded us that we know who God is, our familiar Friend and always warm and close, so very much like us, really.

Most Sunday mornings the sermon is all mercy and no judgment. All blessing and no demand. We no longer imagine God in terrible or capricious terms—that is a good thing and biblically founded—except sometimes we go to the other extreme. We can imagine God as domesticated, a kind of lapdog like man's best friend, always accepting and understanding, always glad to see us, never displeased or demanding. We think of God as our copilot, our rabbit's foot, our personal assistant, or our fire insurance. We see God as our help, but not as our Lord; our last resort, but not our first love. God is a safety net, a secret weapon, a sanctioner, no matter what we set about to do. God so loves us just the way we are, and so there is no mystery, no danger, no call to change or need for repentance.

It is an interesting contrast. In those Puritan days we see sinners in the hands of a too mysterious and capricious God. In these latter days we see a too familiar God in the hands of self-satisfied sinners, capriciously remade in our own image and likeness.

Trinity Sunday and the doctrine it proclaims remind us that God is as near as our breath, but not so familiar as to warrant presumption. God is beyond time and space, but not so mysterious as to be inaccessible or terrifying. We are sinful people, to be sure—and perhaps, when faced with the goodness and power of Jesus, we instinctively and rightly beg Him to depart. But Jesus says, "Do not be afraid. Come, follow Me."

In Jesus' call to Simon, in His call to us, there is the invitation to intimacy, but there is also abiding mystery. Fear gives way to faith, but Simon will never know Jesus completely. When he thinks he does, presumes to challenge Him, he will find himself in the hands of an angry Master.[11]

God is not at our disposal, but rather we are at His. There is always more to God, both His mercy and demand, than we ever completely see or imagine. And that is why Eugene Peterson has said that the Trinity is actually the most practical Christian doctrine of all, and the simplest—this gradually revealed awareness of God's fullness. Father, Son, and Holy Spirit remind us that there is always more of God than we know, always more of God than we can explain, always more of God than we can show. The Trinity says God is not in a box but is bigger, much bigger than we imagine. God is more powerful than we sometimes want to believe or remember, but in remembering it there is great comfort.

William James, the famous American philosopher, used the term *the More* to refer to the Mystery beyond space and time in which all of us live and move and have our being, whether we acknowledge that Mystery or not. Most of the time most of us don't. Instead we live and move and have our being on the familiar and in some ways manageable surface of things.

We live little question to little question—What's for supper? Who won the game? Am I pretty or rich?

Now and then, though, we realize upon what thin ice we tread, how easily the surface can crack and give way. A child gets sick or finds herself in some kind of trouble. A parent dies or betrays us one way or the other. A spouse is no longer interested, and what we had imagined as our lasting worth and value is cast aside as rubbish. Big business proves as heartless as big government, big government proves as selfish and inept as big business. War does not beget peace, only more war, and the Church . . . the Church? Let's just say that the Church does not always practice what it preaches, does not always preach as it should.

Disease comes, or disillusionment. Age is relentless, and so is the Devil. We stroll through our days, most days, just on the surface of things—just strolling along—but then comes the day we stumble or fall, when we scratch the surface of our awareness or it gets ripped wide open. Something or someone, some person or situation, breaks our heart and ruptures our security, and suddenly we find ourselves in the depths, asking ourselves the harder, colder questions of life and faith, of death and hope, of meaning.

We go deeper. We *have* to go deeper to survive, to find the More that is beyond a given space or a given time, to find food that can satisfy us below our immediate hungers or craving, to find that truth to hold like an anchor when all lesser opinions are swept away in the storm. And when we do, we find that the Savior is not only above us but also below us, in us and around us. He is the More who lovingly desires to meet every "I."

I cannot explain the Trinity, this most foundational of our doctrines. It is difficult, a mystery, and all the explanations we have been taught or teach our children are inadequate and even idolatrous: water, ice, steam; apple, peel, core; father, husband, brother. None of that is helpful, not very. But if those things help us begin to see that there is more going on in the world than we can possibly domesticate and more to God than we can ever imagine or manage, more than we can observe or understand, then the little explanations have done their service.

No one can explain it; they can only point to it. I tell the story of my grandmother and her two sisters, and it is not a perfect analogy by any means, but it pleases me to think of the Father, the Son, the Holy Spirit, each of Them and all of Them together fussing over our world, working here and there, sewing, stitching, unstitching, hurting Themselves now and then so that if we know where to look we see the blood stains that prove Their once and future love.

It pleases me to believe there is a cake in the oven too, by which I mean that God is preparing a feast for all His children,[12] and no ingredients are missing. Soon, all of us will dig in and wolf down that delicious eternal confection whose recipe continues to elude our best efforts. Until that day we get up and go to school and we come home again, and some days there seems to be something going on around us, but we cannot yet tell what it is. But there are racks and chairs, conversations and commotion, random movements and haphazard concentrations, and some Day soon we will see that they knew what was going on all along, what God was up to while we were doing other things.

One day soon, there will be a world that will keep us all warm and fed and blessed and at peace. *They* know what They are doing, the Father, the Son, and the Holy Spirit. I believe that. Even now They are stitching and restitching sense and light and purpose into the fabric of our world. *They* are crafting something wondrous, pouring all Their skill and love into the world, making something lasting just for us.

Affirmation: God is Mysterious, Triune, More than we can imagine.

Confession: We try to keep God small, manageable, and thereby miss or ignore the wonder and the blessing of God's fullness.

Discipleship Task: To move from presumptuous familiarity and humbly embrace the mystery of God, who is both beyond us and among us in Jesus.

Advent

Christmas

Epiphany

Lent

Holy Week

Easter

Pentecost

Trinity

Ordinary Time [Corresponds to the Latin term *Tempus per annum* or "time through the year"] : A season of the Christian liturgical calendar comprising two periods—one following Epiphany, the other following Pentecost—which do not fall under the "strong seasons" of Advent, Christmas, Lent, or Easter[1]

Christ the King

Chapter 9

From Boredom to Contentment

Ordinary Time

A child kicks its legs rhythmically through excess, not absence, of life. Because children have abounding vitality, because they are in spirit fierce and free, therefore they want things repeated and unchanged. They always say, "Do it again"; and the grown-up person does it again until he is nearly dead. For grown-up people are not strong enough to exult in monotony. But perhaps God is strong enough. . . . It is possible that God says every morning, "Do it again," to the sun; and every evening, "Do it again," to the moon. It may not be automatic necessity that makes all daisies alike: it may be that God makes every daisy separately, but has never got tired of making them. It may be that He has the eternal appetite of infancy; for we have sinned and grown old, and our Father is younger than we.

— G. K. CHESTERTON

Turn your eyes upon Jesus,
look full in His wonderful face,
And the things of earth will grow strangely dim,
in the light of His glory and grace.

— HELEN LEMMEL

Looking for love in all the wrong places . . .

— MARC ALMOND

It has often been said, as Saint Augustine famously put it, that God has made us for Himself and our hearts find no rest till they rest in Him.[2] There is this God-shaped hole in each of us, and try as we might to fill it with other, lesser things, we are never at peace until that hole is filled with God. We cannot outrun the emptiness any more than we can outrun our own shadow, cannot quench our spiritual thirst unless God does the pouring.

We know that, and many of us are reminded of it time after time. There come moments when we are powerfully reminded both whose and who we are, when we pledge once again to be and become all God created us to be. There come other moments too when we are horribly reminded of life's evanescence, the fragility of our own existence and that of the world. We plead with God, pledge ourselves again to God, know that God alone is eternal refuge and lasting peace. Whether we are blinded by insight or ignorance, we assure ourselves once more in these singular times that what we need is God's to give.

But in between the big moments come other moments, ordinary times, when we all but forget what we know so well, when the ebb and flow of our days hypnotize us into spiritual amnesia, rock us almost to sleep. If we come to again, we discover that we have become discontent, looking elsewhere for refreshment and nourishment and peace, searching in places and things that cannot provide them.

We get bored, distracted from the ordinary presence of God. We crave excitement instead, ground-shaking experiences whether spiritual or not, fireworks. Most often the Lord is not in the earthquakes or fire, but still we can find ourselves turning away from the still, small voice[3] in sleepy deference to other siren voices. Until, that is, there is another significant insight or crisis. Then we go searching again for Jesus, praying He will fill the God-shaped hole once and forever.

We most often live our spiritual lives by fits and starts. Jesus, however, lives His life with constancy, constantly looking to us. His determination to seek and to save that which is lost—namely, us—reveals the "us"-shaped hole in the middle of God's heart. God finds no rest till He is at peace with us, till we are at peace with Him.

We and God lack one thing, and that is each other. If we realize that truth only sometimes, God knows it always, is constantly seeking us for both our sakes.

One day a man came to Jesus asking after eternal life.[4] Maybe he simply meant, "How do I get to Heaven?" or perhaps, "What will make my life meaningful, real?" Of all the New Testament characters, he is the one most like us. We have and still want. We acquire and feel the poorer for it. We fill our lives with many things and yet are barren. The world affords us many distractions, so many diversions, endless entertainment, and we are still bored.

This man too. Whatever his life was filled with, he still felt empty. We recognize in him that one, all-too-familiar hole in each of us.

For Jesus' part, He also loved this man and invited him to be a follower and a friend. In Jesus' call we discern the other and surprising hole, the one in Jesus.

The story ends badly: Both holes remain empty. The man leaves empty and Jesus does too in a way, goes on without him anyway, both of them grieving and traveling their separate ways. The man believed in Jesus, but simply believing wasn't enough. Jesus loved the man, but Jesus' loving him didn't guarantee them relationship or intimacy. And it is so sad. Jesus will continue to seek and to save those who are lost. The man will continue looking for what he has rejected.

We don't even know the man's name. If his answer to Jesus had been different, he might be as well-known to us as Simon or Andrew, James or John. We might remember him as the disciple who was rich but for Jesus' sake gave it all up for the gospel, a foreshadowing of Saint Francis, who gave up the wealth and prestige of his father's legacy in favor of living in a cave and preaching to the birds. All of these incarnated the words of Psalm 19:9-10:

> The ordinances of the LORD are true,
>> and righteous altogether.
> More to be desired are they than gold,
>> even much fine gold.

The Hebrew word translated "desire" is the same word as the one translated "covet" in the Ten Commandments. Thou shalt not covet another's stuff, but thou shalt desire the Lord God. It is both command and reality. We are wired to desire and we will, in fact, want. But sometimes we don't realize how we are wired, don't know what we want. God does, though, and just as Jesus desired the rich man to desire Him more than he did his gold, even if he had much fine gold, God wants us to want God more than anything. God desires to give us Himself more than anything.

The man does not want Jesus that much, however, and turns away. He will not pay this price, even for eternal life. The irony is this: Jesus said what was lacking was that the young man had too much, too many things in his hands to take hold of Jesus.

Jesus didn't fuss. He did not yell or scream or threaten the man with Hell if he refused Jesus' call. There is just this sense of loss. For both of them. Whatever they might have done together, however each might have enriched the other, it is all for naught as the man goes his way and Jesus continues His, never to meet again.

Except, of course, they do. And I wonder what that reunion looked like.

Maybe the man said, "I am sorry, Jesus. I wanted to and couldn't. Forgive me. I am dust." And Jesus would have said, "Of course I forgive you. I loved you then; I love you now. I died for you. Still, I wish you would have come with Me that day." The man would have said, "Me too."

Or maybe the man said this: "You know, I couldn't sleep for weeks thinking about what You said. I kept hearing Your words over and over again in my mind. And so, later, I did what You said. I sold what I had and gave it to the poor. I tried to find You after that, catch up, but I never could. I did my best to follow at a distance, though."

And Jesus would have said, "Well done, good and faithful servant. You proved faithful in a few things . . . late but faithful . . . enter into the joy of your Father's kingdom."

The Church calendar, start to finish, rightly focuses on the big events, the major moments in the story of Jesus—His coming and birth; the visit of the Wise Men; His suffering, death, and resurrection; His appearances to the disciples until His ascension; and then His sending of the Holy Spirit.

What happens in between the big times is not so much unremarkable as it is pedestrian, as workaday as the word *ordinary* connotes. What makes Jesus most interesting during these in-between times is that each day looks like most every other day in Jesus' life, and He is never bored. Frustrated—He is that sometimes, tired and angry too. But He never seems distracted.

It is hard to follow Jesus' example in this way. Jesus is constant, content, never resting really and never stopping. He is God-focused, sure of His mission, unwavering. His ministry is, as Eugene Peterson put it, a "long obedience in the same direction," whether in the big moments or the other moments. He keeps doing what He was sent to do, interruptions and detours notwithstanding.

One time when Jesus had been summoned to the home of Jairus, whose daughter was near death and there was no time to lose, a woman with gynecological problems—she had been bleeding for twelve years—interrupted Jesus, touched Him. He knew it, turned, and said, "Who touched Me?" It was a silly question in a way, for many people were pressed in on Him, but Jesus knew something more was going on. "Who touched Me?" and the woman fessed up.[5] Jesus might have been mad or angry, just as He might have been mad or angry at the leper that morning after all the healings in Capernaum,[6] or at the people following Him around and running ahead to clamor after Him, and He had no time to Himself or to His disciples.[7] Yet He had compassion on all of these, took time to heal, to teach, to feed—true to His mission, interruptions or no.

One of the stories we tell during Ordinary Time—on those Sundays that proceed in *order* between the major commemorations—is the only miracle recorded by all four evangelists, the feeding of the five thousand. In Matthew Jesus feeds five thousand *men*, which may mean there were altogether three or four times that many in this crowd that kept following Jesus: twenty thousand people, maybe. That number is interesting because, by the end of John 6, the crowds have all left to go looking, we assume, for someone or something else to fill their empty stomachs. The defection is so absolute that only the Twelve are left, and Jesus asks if they too want to leave, to go back to their homes and families, their old way of life.

It was Passover, John tells us,[8] a time to remember how Moses led the people out of Egypt. Jesus looked a little like Moses, only Jesus walked on the water instead of parting the sea. Jesus did not provide the hungry people manna or water from a rock, but His own flesh and blood. It was Passover, but it was different too.

Jesus is a prophet like Moses, but more. He is a King, but other than and different from David. His teaching taxed the imagination of the restless, hungry people, for He demanded that they think beyond their stomachs. Yes, they were hungry, but they needed so much more than bread. He was making a point, teaching a lesson, feeding them less out of compassion and more by way of instruction, trying to show His disciples and the crowds that He Himself *is* the provision of God, the meaning and purpose of their lives and of all history beyond the momentary.

"I am the Bread of Life," Jesus said. "I Myself am the manna, but more, other, different, better. The bread the Israelites ate all those generations ago, it perished as they themselves did in the wilderness. The bread you ate just awhile ago—what's in your belly and what's left of it in these baskets—it too perishes, goes stale, feeds the earth or feeds the birds or not at all. People who eat *only* this food likewise perish. But if anyone eats My flesh, which is bread indeed, and drinks My blood, which is drink indeed, he will never die. I am the *living* bread," Jesus said.[9]

We hear His words and think of the Eucharist. The people heard His words and weren't sure what to think. "How can this man give us his flesh to eat?" they whispered.[10] They were thinking literally, physically, but Jesus wanted them to think metaphorically, sacramentally, beneath the obvious. He would be their nourishment, their food and drink. He alone could and would fill the empty place, offered them a salvation they could not yet imagine.

And so they turned away, many of them, confronted as they were and confounded by this lesson. It was among Jesus' hardest teachings and remains so to this pluralistic day: that this one particular man living at this one particular time is God's once and ever unique means of eternal salvation; only by coming to *Him*, eating and drinking of Him, do any of God's children find the contentment they crave and need.

Many that day had come only for a meal and perhaps a miracle, for the bread and circuses. What they got in addition was a blunt tutorial, and so the crowds circled back and went away. And *even some of His disciples,* John tells us, *some of His chosen and called,* turned away and no longer followed Him.

Some days I can understand. I want to consider myself a disciple, but so many of Jesus' teachings are hard. Day after ordinary day, hating one's life in this world to save it for the next;[11] loving one's enemies[12] — one's *enemies* — and forgiving one's friends[13] (which in some ways is the harder, more demanding work); sacrificing for another when I am so well-schooled in looking out for myself.[14]

Following Jesus is not always satisfying in most of the ways we count satisfaction. We might rather opt to love our stuff and hate our enemies. We might rather live for the day or to advance our own purposes. We might rather keep our gold and turn away from Jesus' command and invitation, even if the hole threatens to swallow us.

Following Jesus is hard. It is hard at all times and harder still in the ordinary moments and times of our lives. It is easier to quit paying attention, to look away, to pretend we didn't hear. It is easier to doze through Jesus' daily sermons than to take Him at His word. No wonder, then, that many of His disciples, then and now, though they began to follow Him, turn away when the teaching gets rough and look for other instructors and counsel by which to live.

But there are some who know already that the wisdom of the world is a confection, as airy as mousse. Other teachers do not give us faith, hope, or love enough to shoulder real life or real death. When life kicks us in the shins or breaks our hearts, when we are bored with life as it is and forced to confess how little we can do to improve it, where shall we go, whom should see about that? Simon Peter knows.

When the crowds had left, Jesus turned to His twelve closest friends and asked them, "Do you also wish to go away?" In good rabbinical fashion, though he was no rabbi, Simon asked Jesus a question in turn: "Lord, to whom shall we go?"

Simon's query was more than rhetoric. Before Jesus could say another word, Simon answered his own question for the Teacher and for the Twelve and for the rest of us too: "You have the words of eternal life; and we have believed, and have come to know, that you are the Holy One of God."[15]

Affirmation: Jesus comes to us in the ordinary moments of life.

Confession: We are easily bored and so turn back or look elsewhere for fulfillment.

Discipleship Task: To stay with Jesus in the ordinary moments of our lives, to feed on Him as our daily bread, to rejoice in His peace as our contentment.

Advent

Christmas

Epiphany

Lent

Holy Week

Easter

Pentecost

Trinity

Ordinary Time

Christ the King 1: Christ the King Sunday celebrates the all-embracing authority of Christ as
King and Lord of the cosmos. Officially called
the Feast of Our Lord Jesus Christ the King, it is
celebrated on the final Sunday of Ordinary Time,
the Sunday before Advent[1]

Chapter 10

From Faith to Sight

Christ the King

Born thy people to deliver, born a child and yet a king
Born to reign in us for ever, now thy gracious kingdom bring.
By thine own eternal spirit, rule in all our hearts alone.
By thine all sufficient merit, raise us to thy glorious throne.

— CHARLES WESLEY

It seemed to Us that peace could not be more effectually restored nor fixed upon a firmer basis than through the restoration of the Empire of Our Lord. We were led in the meantime to indulge the hope of a brighter future at the sight of a more widespread and keener interest evinced in Christ and his Church, the one Source of Salvation, a sign that men who had formerly spurned the rule of our Redeemer and had exiled themselves from his kingdom were preparing, and even hastening, to return to the duty of obedience.

— POPE PIUS XI

One afternoon when I was in college, I remember stopping by my father's office in a section of Nashville we called Green Hills. It was a little room in the basement beside the back stairs of a two-story building—barely large enough for two drawing boards and my father. He had landed there after a tumultuous period in his professional life. Months before he had been in a second-floor suite, with four employees and a good engineering business, so good that he had been bought out by a larger firm downtown. He went to work for the new owners, making more and more regularly than he ever had, but the time clock and the strictures of being an employee quickly began to chafe. What had seemed the promised land at last—steady hours and a steady paycheck—soon felt like wilderness and exile, and so he quit the new firm, left his former employees there, and went back to the basement of his old building, alone and with few clients. And there I found him one afternoon.

We did not talk about his business; we talked about his soul. Perhaps the peaks and valleys of recent days had left him uncertain, unsure of God's will or way or purposes in his life. The outward stuff was making my father look inward, to ask whether God is, or whether God cares. My father was in crisis, could not see the way forward.

I will never forget what he asked me: "Have you ever wondered if you really were saved?" The question stunned me. I had given my eight-year-old life to Jesus sitting on Daddy's knee. Surely he had not forgotten. Or was he conducting a test, one last experiment, and if I said "yes" right away, it might have been the end of him, proof positive of his absolute dereliction—God was not with him then and never had been.

Or maybe he was asking me not father to son at all but preacher to preacher. I was serving a small congregation in Nashville, God help them, as my father had served several through the years. Suddenly it dawned on me that what he really was asking was this: "After preaching deliverance to the captives, have you ever wondered whether you yourself might be a castaway?"[2]

Is it true, after all, what we preach and believe and proclaim? True not only for those who hear it but also for those who preach it? Is this Jesus the One, the One for all so that all may find in this One hope and love and, until we can see, faith? Jews and Gentiles, slave and free, rich and poor, men and women?

Paul wondered the same thing, of course. So did the prophet Elijah and John Wesley, founder of the Methodist Church, and John the Baptist too.

Seven hundred years after the time of Isaiah, another prophet appeared among the people of Israel, dressed in skins and leather and with bugs in his teeth. John appeared in the wilderness, and many went to see for themselves what had appeared. They had heard of prophets but had never seen one, at least not like John. He preached repentance and baptism, and many were baptized as a sign of their desire for cleansing. John himself desired cleansing, confessed as much when he saw Jesus wading toward him in the water. He saw more besides: "Behold, the Lamb of God!"[3] he said one day to his own disciples, two of whom left John to follow Jesus.

Only now, John was in a different kind of wilderness. He was in prison and was sending some friends to Jesus to ask a question: "Are you the one who is to come, or are we to wait for another?"[4]

It is a terribly poignant question, a critical moment in the

Gospels (and not altogether unlike that day in Green Hills in my dad's office): the preacher, his strength for preaching almost gone and unsure of what he has been preaching all these years. It happens.

So John sent some friends to Jesus, who takes away the sin of the world, in hopes that Jesus could maybe take away the doubt in his heart. If Jesus was the way and the truth and the life, then imprisonment and even death at the hands of Herod was no real threat. If Jesus was not all these things, then imprisonment and even death at the hands of Herod might be a relief, an end to his disillusioned hopes.

But how would John know for sure? He could not judge by what his eyes saw because he was in prison and unable to see much of anything. In fact, John was only able to judge by what his ears heard, by what his friends and disciples told him.

Jesus said to them, "Go tell John what *you* see and hear, that there is healing going on and that should be proof enough. Blind folks get sight and deaf folks get sound and the poor are blessed by the preaching of good news. If you believe me, and if you tell what you believe, John will believe you and trust me. His faith will be restored, prison or no, and your faith will be rewarded and everyone will get happy if no one takes offense."[5]

John was waiting for a word from his friends; he would believe if they believed. My father was waiting in his office for a word from me, and he would believe if I believed.

All around us are people waiting, and they will believe if we believe, but sometimes we too are waiting—are in prisons of one kind or another, whether of disappointments or regrets or grief, of anger or pride or prejudice. Perhaps it is we who cannot see Jesus right now, for whatever reason.

But if our friends told us that, yes, it is all of it true, that they can see as they never saw before, can hear things they never heard, then maybe we could trust them and begin to believe again that what we have said and sung and maybe even taught all these years really is the truth after all. Not just for some but for all, and if not altogether now then eventually. Eventually.

If we begin to believe again, then those who are looking to us can begin to believe again a little too, and they will be able to tell their friends in prison that, yes, it is all of it true, this gospel of Jesus Christ.

We really do believe. That is what John's disciples told him not long before he died. And that is what I told my poor, old father not long before he died. I told him in just the same way he had told it so often to me. "Yes, Daddy, you can believe this gospel. You can trust this One. Soon, all will be set right. Soon we will all live in the light. Soon there will come a shoot of hope from the dead stump of our hearts. Faith will be sight. Soon, and very soon."

I had believed the Good News about Jesus when Dad told it to me, and I believe he believed it, or believed it again, when I told him that afternoon. Yes, we can all of us believe, trust, what we have so often told each other, that Jesus is the Way and the Truth and the Life. He comes to us in our every wilderness, keeps coming, that we might follow and come to Him at last.

It is all one Story, really, the Good News of Jesus Christ, the Son of God.[6] Jesus' friends are telling us they have seen and heard, and they are telling us we can believe, can trust, can have faith in this Jesus till we have eyes at last to see Him for ourselves. We will see Him—the Scriptures' promise is clear[7]—but until we do, we can trust those who have been with Him.

The Story they tell us is a great narrative arc looping back on itself, year after year. Start anywhere and eventually you will go everywhere. Open your New Testament to Matthew, say, or Luke, and before you are done, you will have read Mark and John. Close your eyes, flip the pages, drop your finger on a text, and eventually you will trace all the other texts, the Braille-like textures of the next episode or the previous saying.

Come with Jesus to the riverside, and you will go with Him to the Sea of Galilee. Follow Him into the home of Simon Peter, or Simon the Leper, and you will soon be a guest in Bethany, as well, in the home of Mary and Martha and Lazarus. Go with Jesus, cheering, to Jerusalem, and you will come with Him, weeping, to Gethsemane, and after that fearfully to the courtyard of Caiaphas, the palace of Pilate, the court of Herod, and the hill called Calvary. Die with Him and you will be raised with Him; love His appearing and you will see His departing, His ascension, but also His return.

Bethlehem's manger, Nazareth's synagogue, Olivet's prow, the Garden's tomb, the New Jerusalem — it is all of it one geography, really, one place, where God meets us in Jesus, where Heaven meets earth. Begin with the Beginning and you will come to the End; begin here at the End, Christ the King, and you will come back to the Beginning. He came; He is coming. He was promised; He is expected. His birth breaks all time into before and after. His life breaks up every pretense and convention. His death breaks down every ethnic hostility, destroys every racial barrier, gathers every people into one people. His judgment scatters, separates, divides. His grace forgives, restores, unites.

It is all one Story, the Story of Jesus — but with many episodes, many chapters, many discreet characterizations. He creates the world.[8] He cannot create faith.[9] He is a healer,[10] and He is helpless.[11] He is the giver of life[12] and the victim of murder.[13] He is seen after His death,[14] but not by everyone. He is all one Jesus, the very One about whom a many-faceted Story is told.

Invoke any of His names—Rabbi, Master, Faithful Witness, Firstborn of the Dead, Lord or Lamb, Ruler of the kings of the earth—and eventually you will call Him by all of His names, will crown Him with many crowns, will pray to Him all your prayers, will praise Him for all His works.

Among Jesus' many names and appellations are these: the King of kings and Lord of lords.[15] The word *king* rasps in modern ears, and so too does *lord*. Many moderns consider such terms ciphers of oppression and patriarchy, easy encryptions for crusades and hypocrisy, and they reject Jesus outright, if only because Christians call Him King and Lord.

To say Christ is King is not to suggest that Jesus is like other kings, who are either tyrants or gods, jokers or jesters, anachronisms and, on account of their silliness and celebrity, impotent potentates.

No, to say that Christ is the King of kings and Lord of lords is to say that He is first of all because He is "servant of all."[16] To say Christ is King is to remember how, over and over again, He took His place with sinners and riffraff, ate with outcasts and touched lepers. He came not to be served but to serve.

To say Christ is King is to remember how, when He comes out of the tomb, He does not charge the halls of Pilate or the courts of Herod but instead takes a Sunday afternoon walk with two of His disciples, who have no idea who He is but need to see, and so, no surprise, when He begins to break the bread and serve the wine, they recognize Him.

Whenever Jesus was offered a high position He took the lower seat instead, kneeling to pray, to wash His disciples' feet, to be nailed to a cross. He lived and died to serve, and He lives again for exactly the same reasons—to save and serve His chosen, His children.

To say that Christ is King is to say that His kingdom is not of this world—you cannot take a train there. His kingdom is on the map of every human heart, a destination toward which all God's children journey, lost and detoured though they seem to be. It is the reign of God among those whose hearts are on the way to the Land that has been promised, wandering and wayfaring though they sometimes feel they are. Christ is Lord of all who love Him and even those who don't; He is King of this world, though His reign some days seems all but hidden, and He is the King of the world to come.

When peace is made, when repentance is preached and forgiveness experienced, when the hungry are fed and the homeless housed, when the powerful are brought down from their thrones and the meek inherit the earth—here and there, now and then, we begin to see a little of what will One Day be Everywhere and for Always: Christ, "all in all."[17]

Until then, Sunday by Sunday, season by season, year by year, we proclaim this End as our starting point, this faith as the Beginning of our sight. This promise is the premise of our worship, this consummation our invitation to sing, to pray, to receive, and to give: Jesus Christ, the Alpha and the Omega, the First and the Last, the Once and Coming and Eternal King.

All we say of Jesus, all we claim about Him and for Him, all we pledge of ourselves to Him draws its meaning from this End. Saint Julian, a crazy old saint, had a vision of the End that she could only describe this way: "And all shall be well. And all shall be well. And all manner of things shall be well." It was, I think, her way of saying Christ is King. Has been, will be, and therefore is. The end of our faith is also its beginning, and its beginnings already prefigure the End: Christ is King.

In 1934, Karl Barth and others of the confessing Church in Germany published the Barmen Declaration, a thunderous proclamation of the primacy of Christ as a denunciation of all this-worldly usurpers and pretenders to His throne. Hitler and the state church that supported his Reich were the primary targets of Barth and his colleagues, but their "yes" to Jesus was a "no" to many other Christ-pretending leaders.

Nine years before the Barmen Declaration, in 1925, Pope Pius XI inaugurated the Feast of Christ the King as a doxological celebration of the same truth.[18] If Barmen's prophetic declaration offered pastoral comfort to those endangered by the Nazis and their court prophets, the priestly feast constituted prophetic liturgy—a diminution of the powers and principalities that war for our allegiance.

Both Barmen and the feast have as their heart this one impulse, to exalt Christ and Christ alone, to shame the lesser powers of earth, to remind all disciples, all along their various journeys, that their first, last, and abiding allegiance is to Christ. That His abiding allegiance is to us.

On the wall of my study is a framed picture my son Jacob drew of me when he was about four. My body is a line and my arms another line crossing my body at more or less right angles. My legs are short sticks. It is a wonder I can stand or keep my balance. My head is a big circle with a crooked smile stretched across one side of my face and a few uneven teeth. I am wearing some kind of hat. At the end of each of my stick arms is a ball—these are my hands and each of them sprouts fifteen or seventeen fingers, little lines coming out all sorts of ways. I am tilting to the side a bit. Or perhaps Jacob has already mastered forced perspective and I am leaning toward him for a hug. I hope what he remembers as he draws is a loving, not menacing, intrusion into his space.

Above the picture are letters—my wife, Jo, told me later how she wrapped her own hand around Jacob's and helped him form the crayon words—"My Dad." It is not the most recognizable or accurate picture ever made of me, but because it was drawn with love it is the most precious.

The Church wraps its hands around ours and helps us write our words, for when it comes to drawing our pictures of Jesus, all the various portraits His life and work inspire us to draw, I suspect that even our most objective and studied efforts still look, to His eyes, more or less like that picture in my office. But we keep drawing them, remembering how He is coming toward us in love. Our little pictures proclaim our love of Him and remind us of His allegiance to us—His forever and always promise to be with us, come what may. And we in turn promise to stay with Him, come what may, until He comes at last.

We remind ourselves that although all we can sometimes see with our natural eyes are the tyrants, dictators, false prophets, and fearsome pretenders, theirs is not the last word or the lasting power. When we are afraid, when the voices whisper in our ears that we must acquiesce, go along, give the Devil his due—it is in those times especially that we must remember our stories, draw our pictures, hold fast our hope and sing, even with quavering voice,

This is my Father's world.
O let me ne'er forget
that though the wrong seems oft so strong,
God is the ruler yet.
This is my Father's world:
why should my heart be sad?
The Lord is King; let the heavens ring!
God reigns; let the earth be glad![19]

Soon and very soon light will at last cleave the cold, dark pall draped over the broken earth and its poor, miserable creatures, the befuddling gloom that smothers the hearts and minds of God's children. The thick clouds of doubt and war that have hidden the heavens and dimmed our vision were stabbed through at Bethlehem, but their complete dissipation is now at hand. We have been waiting a long time.

Till that Morning, we sing. Till we see, we believe. Till we know, we tell to all those who are imprisoned that we do believe in God, we do trust in Jesus His Christ, who is and who was and who will be, the coming One and Savior of the world, the once and future King of the universe, blessed be He. His Holy Spirit is among us even now as power and comfort and peace.

That is a Story to tell to the nations, a song to sing in the night, a word to calm the fears and quicken the steps of every journeying disciple, of every pilgrim soul.

Affirmation: Jesus comes to us as the Once and Future King.

Confession: We do not always see Jesus and doubt His reign.

Discipleship Task: To worship and proclaim that Christ is King till we move from faith to sight.

Notes

Introduction:
Jesus Calls, Disciples Follow

1. Luke 3:4.
2. Based on Baruch 5:7; Isaiah 40:3-5; see also Luke 3:5-6.
3. See John 1:14.
4. 1 John 3:2.
5. Lauren Winner (lecture, WNCC Order of the Elders, Kanuga Conference Center, Hendersonville, NC, November 13, 2006).

Chapter 1:
Promises in the Dark (Advent)

1. See Genesis 1:5,8,13,19,23,31.
2. See Lamentations 3:23.
3. I use *holy* here in the sense of "set apart," not as morally faultless or, as we sometimes incorrectly say, "saintly."
4. Isaiah 11:1-2.
5. Isaiah 11:3-4, free rendering.
6. Psalm 85:10.

CHAPTER 2:
GOD WITH US (CHRISTMAS)

1. See Luke 1:6.
2. Luke 1:18, free rendering.
3. See Luke 1:26-28.
4. Luke 1:35, free rendering.
5. The Greek word is translated among Orthodox and Catholic Christians as "Mother of God," granting special recognition to Mary. The literal rendering is "God-bearer," a designation given by Jesus to everyone who has faith (see Mark 3:34).
6. See 2 Timothy 4:8.
7. See Mark 3:35.
8. Based on Luke 4:16-19; compare Isaiah 58:6 and 61:1-2.
9. Luke 1:46-49.
10. Luke 1:43, free rendering.
11. Luke 1:51-53, free rendering.
12. See, for example, the "Infancy Gospels," in Montague Rhodes James, *The Apocryphal New Testament* (Oxford: The Clarendon Press, 1924–1975), 88–89.
13. We see this pattern in several Old Testament stories, most clearly in the story of Hannah and Samuel (1 Samuel 1:1-20).
14. For theological and historical reasons, Roman Catholic and Eastern Orthodox Christians maintain that Mary remained a virgin her whole life. Scholars in these traditions rightly note that "firstborn son" does not necessarily imply other sons and that the Greek term for "brother" or "sister" (see Mark 3:34, for example) can be translated "cousin" or even "fellow citizen." Most Protestants are unbothered by the notion of Mary having other children — such as James, the "brother of Jesus," who while not an original member of the Twelve comes to be head of the church in Jerusalem (see Acts 15:13-21).

15. W. H. Auden, "For the Time Being," in *Collected Poems*, ed. Edward Mendelson (New York: Random House, 1976), 280.
16. 2 Corinthians 4:18, nrsv.
17. See Luke 2:1-3.
18. See Matthew 1:25.
19. Ann Weems, *Psalms of Lament* (Louisville: Westminster/John Knox, 1995), xvii; based on Romans 12:5.
20. See Romans 8:22.
21. John 1:46, free rendering.
22. Acts 7:60.
23. See Luke 23:34.
24. John 1:14.
25. Isaiah 9:6-7, nrsv.

Chapter 3:
From an Exclusive to an Inclusive Faith (Epiphany)

1. See Ephesians 1:5.
2. See Ephesians 1:10.
3. Genesis 12:2-3, nrsv.
4. See Ezra 10:2-5, for example; see also Joshua 6:15-21.
5. See Isaiah 25:6-9.
6. See the book of Jonah.
7. Isaiah 49:6.
8. See Isaiah 55:5.
9. Whatever or whoever else Isaiah might have had in mind—a new political or military leader, even an ideal high priest—we see Jesus, a Light of revelation to the Gentiles and a glory for Israel.
10. Mark 4:33-34, nrsv.
11. Luke 15:4, free rendering.
12. See Luke 15:9.

13. See Matthew 13:3-9.

14. See Luke 15:22-30.

15. See Matthew 9:17.

16. See Matthew 13:44.

17. See Matthew 13:31.

18. See Matthew 13:33.

19. See John 3:5.

20. See Matthew 10:39.

21. See John 3:8.

22. Emily Dickinson, "Tell all the Truth but tell it slant," http://nongae.gsnu.ac.kr/~songmu/Poetry/TellAllTheTruthButTEllItSlant.htm.

> Tell all the Truth but tell it slant—
> Success in Cirrcuit lies
> Too bright for our infirm Delight
> The Truth's superb surprise
> As Lightening to the Children eased
> With explanation kind
> The Truth must dazzle gradually
> Or every man be blind—

23. See Mark 4:30-32.

24. See Mark 13:28.

25. See Mark 12:1-9.

26. Mark 3:5, free rendering.

27. See Mark 1:40.

28. Mark 1:38, free rendering.

29. Mark 1:40-41, NRSV.

30. Those with study Bibles can check the footnotes at Mark 1:41 to see that many Greek manuscripts read that Jesus' emotional reaction to the leper's request was anger.

31. See Mark 1:9 and parallels.

32. See Psalm 1:3.
33. Matthew 3:15, NRSV.
34. Matthew 4:1-11; Mark 1:12-13; Luke 4:1-13, free rendering.
35. See Matthew 14:13-21; Mark 6:34-44; Luke 9:10-17; and John 6:1-15.
36. Mark 1:14-15.
37. Luke 6:23-25, free rendering.
38. Matthew 5:11, free rendering.
39. Matthew 12:30, free rendering.
40. Mark 9:40, free rendering.
41. Matthew 5:21,27,33,38,43, free rendering.
42. Based on John 15:15.
43. Mark 1:29.
44. See Matthew 13:47.
45. Mark 9:2-8 and parallels.
46. See Mark 6:7.
47. Mark 9:38.
48. Mark 9:19, free rendering.
49. John 13:1.

Chapter 4:
From Entitlement to Selflessness (Lent)

1. Luke 2:29, NRSV.
2. Luke 2:30-32, NRSV.
3. Based on John 15:18; Luke 9:23.
4. See Luke 12:16-21.
5. Philippians 2:6-8, free rendering.
6. Johnson is the modern-day equivalent of Bar-Jona, or "son of John."
7. Matthew 16:13-17 and parallels.
8. Mark 8:31-32.

9. Matthew 6:24, NRSV.
10. 2 Corinthians 8:9, free rendering.
11. See Mark 9:35.
12. See Matthew 20:21.
13. Matthew 10:39, free rendering.
14. Luke 4:18-19; compare Isaiah 58:6 and 61:1-2.
15. Mark 3:6, KJV.

Chapter 5:
From Fear to Surrender (Holy Week)

1. See Mark 10:32.
2. Luke 9:51.
3. Luke 22:42.
4. Luke 9:44.
5. Matthew 21:5, NRSV.
6. Luke 19:37.
7. See Matthew 27:51.
8. See John 2:13-22.
9. John 2:17; compare Psalm 69:9.
10. John 2:16, emphasis added.
11. John 2:19.
12. See Matthew 21:1-9; Mark 11:1-10; Luke 19:28-44.
13. Matthew 21:13, NKJV.
14. John 12:23-26, NRSV.
15. John 12:27, NRSV.
16. See John 11:1-3.
17. John 11:16, NRSV.
18. See John 12:32.
19. See Luke 4:6-8.
20. See John 6:15.
21. See Luke 19:38.

22. See, for example, 1 Samuel 10:1.
23. See John 12:1-8.
24. John 12:4-5, free rendering.
25. Matthew 19:21, free rendering.
26. See Matthew 26:8.
27. John 12:8, free rendering.
28. See Matthew 26:14; Mark 14:10.
29. See Luke 22:3; John 13:27.
30. See Matthew 27:3-5.
31. The accounts by Matthew and Luke differ. See Matthew 27:5 and Acts 1:18.
32. Matthew 22:37-39.
33. John 13:34, free rendering.
34. See John 13:1.
35. A mixture of apples, raisins, and nuts that recalls the mortar used by Egyptian slaves to build the pyramids. See Pastor Michael Smith and Rabbi Rami Shapiro, *Let Us Break Bread Together: A Passover Haggadah for Christians* (Brewster, MA: Paraclete, 2005), xviii.
36. Luke 22:19-20 and parallels, free rendering.
37. John 13:12-15, free rendering.
38. See Matthew 26:38-44 and parallels.
39. John 19:7-8.
40. See Luke 23:8-9.
41. See Mark 6:16.
42. See Matthew 26:65.
43. See John 11:50.
44. See John 18:15.
45. John 19:5, free rendering.
46. See John 19:11.
47. Hebrews 9:22.
48. See Luke 23:32-43.

49. Luke 23:39.
50. Luke 23:43.
51. Simone Weil, in *Waiting for God*, cited in Rueben P. Job and Norman Shawchuck, eds., *A Guide to Prayer for Ministers and Other Servants* (Nashville: The Upper Room, 1983), 114.
52. See Romans 7:19-20.
53. Compare John 12:26.

CHAPTER 6:
FROM SKEPTICISM TO BELIEF (EASTER DAY AND SEASON)

1. John 11:24.
2. See John 11:43.
3. See Mark 5:41.
4. See Luke 7:14.
5. Mark 8:31, free rendering.
6. John 11:25.
7. See John 20:8-10. The context implies their belief in Mary's word, not in the fact of the Resurrection.
8. See Luke 24:12.
9. John 20:19-29, free rendering.
10. 1 Corinthians 15:14-19, free rendering.
11. Acts 3:17-19, free rendering.

CHAPTER 7:
FROM WAITING TO WITNESS (PENTECOST)

1. See Acts 1:11.
2. See John 20:19.
3. See Luke 24:30-31.
4. See Luke 24:36.
5. Acts 1:3, NRSV.

6. Matthew 28:17.
7. Acts 1:8, NRSV.
8. LUKE 24:49, NRSV.
9. LUKE 24:49, NKJV.
10. Acts 1:4-5, NRSV.
11. Acts 1:8, NRSV.
12. See Acts 1:12-14.
13. See Mark 7:31-37.
14. See John 9:6.
15. This sentiment comes famously from the lips of John Wesley, who, as he returned to England on a storm-tossed boat after a failed attempt at missionary work among Native Americans and English expatriates in Georgia, confessed to God his misery: "I came to America to convert the Indians; who, O God, will convert me?"
16. James 3:1.
17. Cited in Kathleen Norris, *The Cloister Walk* (New York: Riverhead Books, 1996), 363.

CHAPTER 8:
FROM FAMILIARITY TO MYSTERY (TRINITY SUNDAY)

1. But see Romans 8:9-11; 1 Corinthians 12:4-7; Matthew 28:19.
2. John 1:1,3, free rendering.
3. See Isaiah 55:8.
4. See Isaiah 1:18.
5. See John 15:14.
6. See Romans 8:16.
7. Luke 4:22.
8. Mark 6:3, free rendering.
9. Luke 5:8, NRSV.

10. Edwards' sermon can be found in many places, including http://www.ccel.org/e/edwards/sermons/sinners.html.
11. See Mark 8:31-33.
12. See Isaiah 25:6-9.

Chapter 9:
From Boredom to Contentment (Ordinary Time)

1. Wikipedia, s.v. "Ordinary Time," http://en.wikipedia.org/wiki/Ordinary_Time.
2. Saint Augustine, *The Confessions*, book 1, paragraph 1, trans. Maria Boulding, OSB, Vintage Spiritual Classics (New York: Vintage, 1997), 3. Boulding's rendering of Saint Augustine's Latin is, "Our heart is unquiet until it rests in you."
3. See 1 Kings 19:9-12.
4. See Mark 10:17-22.
5. Mark 5:21-34, free rendering.
6. See Mark 1:41; see also pages 66–67.
7. See Mark 6:30-31.
8. See John 6:4.
9. John 6:48-51, free rendering.
10. John 6:52.
11. See John 12:25.
12. See Matthew 5:44.
13. See Luke 17:1-4.
14. See John 15:13.
15. John 6:67-69.

Chapter 10:
From Faith to Sight (Christ the King)

1. "All About Christ the King Sunday," ChurchYear.Net, http://www.churchyear.net/ctksunday.html.
2. Based on 1 Corinthians 9:27.
3. John 1:36.
4. Luke 7:19, nrsv.
5. Luke 7:22-23, free rendering.
6. See Mark 1:1.
7. See 1 John 3:2.
8. See John 1:3.
9. See Mark 6:6.
10. See Matthew 17:14-18.
11. See Mark 15:34.
12. See John 11:44.
13. See Mark 15:22-37.
14. See John 20:11-23.
15. See Revelation 19:16; see also 1 Timothy 6:15.
16. Mark 9:35.
17. Ephesians 1:23.
18. Pope Pius XI, "Quas Primas (On the Feast of Christ the King)," December 11, 1925, http://www.ewtn.com/library/encyc/p11prima.htm.
19. Maltbie D. Babcock, "This Is My Father's World," 1901.

About the Author

THOMAS R. (Tom) STEAGALD (STEE-gald) is the pastor of First United Methodist Church (http://fumcstan.com) in Stanley, North Carolina. He is a popular speaker, has written three books (most recently *Praying for Dear Life*, also from NavPress, 2006), and for eight years was a featured columnist for the *Marshville Home News*. His numerous articles and reviews have appeared in *The Christian Century*, *Circuit Rider* (print and electronic), *Lectionary Homiletics*, *Biblical Preaching Journal*, *The Abingdon Preaching Annual*, and the WJK *Lectionary Commentary* series. Tom has studied at Belmont University, The Southern Baptist Theological Seminary, Wake Forest University, and Candler School of Theology at Emory University (DMin). He and Jo, his wife of twenty-four years, are the proud parents of Bethany, a graduate student in Christian ethics, and Jacob, a college sophomore. Presiding over their entire clan is Chester, an English bulldog. Tom's blog site is http://prayerpilgrimage.blogspot.com/.

CHECK OUT THESE OTHER GREAT TITLES FROM NAVPRESS!